AS I SEE
RELIGION

AS I SEE RELIGION

by

HARRY
EMERSON
FOSDICK

GREENWOOD PRESS, PUBLISHERS
WESTPORT, CONNECTICUT

Library of Congress Cataloging in Publication Data

Fosdick, Harry Emerson, 1878-1969.
   As I see religion.

   Reprint of the ed. published by Harper, New York.
   Bibliography: p.
   1.   Religion.   I.   Title.
BL48.F6   1975   200'.1   75-11835
ISBN 0-8371-8142-9

Originally published in 1932 by Harper & Brothers Publishers,
New York

Reprinted with the permission of Harper & Row, Publishers, Inc.

Reprinted in 1975 by Greenwood Press,
a division of Williamhouse-Regency Inc.

Library of Congress Catalog Card Number 75-11835

ISBN 0-8371-8142-9

Printed in the United States of America

CONTENTS

What Is Religion?

THE elusiveness of religion puzzles many people. Once they could describe it with definiteness and finality as identical with their creed and church. With widening horizons, however, religion has become ambiguous. It includes Christ and Buddha, Lao-tse and Mary Baker G. Eddy. It takes in polytheist, monotheist, and humanist. Bishop Manning, Billy Sunday, Gandhi, Professor Whitehead at Harvard, and Voliva of Zion City are all religious. Many, therefore, who began by believing in religion have first fallen into doubt about it, and now are not so much either believing or doubting as wondering what it is.

Science has been described as the art of giving the same name to different things:..by which is meant that considering black coal, white paper, red apples, green leaves, and colorless gasoline, it requires science to reveal that they all are chiefly carbon. What, then, shall be said about the strange incongruities which comprehensively are called religion? Fetish-worship in Africa and Fundamentalism in the United States; Hindus chanting "Om" before the vast impersonal Absolute, and Christians seeking gifts from a highly individualized Father; Shinto priests and Mohammedan mahdis; Quakers and popes; William Jennings Bryan and John Haynes Holmes—what common element can make one thing, religion, of such a salmagundi?

When the intelligentsia try to clarify this situation by their definitions they only confound it the more. If anyone, confused about religion's meaning, wishes to make his bewilderment more complete, let him become a connoisseur in definitions of religion. Matthew Arnold called it "morality touched by emotion"; Professor Tylor, "the belief in Spiritual Beings." Professor Whitehead describes it as "what the individual does with his own solitariness"; but Professor Ames calls it "the pursuit on the part of the community, or the individual member of the community, of what are thought to be the highest social values." Professor Stratton defines it as "man's whole bearing toward what seems to him the Best, or Greatest"; while Professor Lowie sees its essence in the "sense of something transcending the expected or natural, a sense of the Extraordinary, Mysterious, or Supernatural." Salomon Reinach thinks it is "a sum of scruples which impede the free exercise of our faculties"; but Professor Haydon exalts it as "the co-operative quest for a completely satisfying life." To George Bernard Shaw religion is "that which binds men to one another and irreligion that which sunders"; while Havelock Ellis writes, "Now and again we must draw a deep breath of relief—and that is religion." After which, and a great deal more of the same sort, one moves the previous question: What is religion?

That this inquiry, so far from being merely theoretical, is of practical importance, anyone acquainted with the younger generation in its lucid and serious intervals will testify. One cannot sell them a foregone conclusion in religion any more. They will not repeat theological shibboleths or accept partisan church loyalties, supposing them to be religion. They do not any longer believe, to use one girl's phrase, that "God is a Baptist." They know too much about the protean exhibitions of religion in history, and the immense and sometimes splendid reaches of spiritual life which the historic Jesus never influenced, to have the old denominational patriotisms or even the old Christian formulas passed off on them as necessarily bona fide religion. Yet they are religious; at least, they are intensely interested in religion; and as they face the world's potpourri of faiths, above their mingled belief and doubt one feels their increasing wonder as to what, after all, religion is.

This chapter does not propose further to confuse the tangled situation by another endeavor to define religion. Nor shall I seek, as so many have sought, some irreducible minimum that, like carbon in sweet sugar and in bitter strychnine, makes one substance of all faiths from Shintoism to Christian Science. What I should like to do is to describe the approach to religion's meaning which especially characterizes our own time and which is bound to have an important influence upon the religious thought and life of our children.

II

Religion is increasingly dealt with to-day not in ecclesiastical or theological, but in psychological terms. Increasing numbers of people mean by religion, not first of all a true church or an orthodox system of theology, but a psychological experience. There, they think, lies the germinal nucleus of the matter; and this conviction makes a serious difference between them and many historic definers of religion.

The whole discussion, for example, whose bitterness makes a controversial waste of so much so-called Christian history, as to which is the true church, seems to this school of thought a poor expenditure of time because there is no such thing as a true church. All religious organizations, like all secular organizations, are approximate endeavors to meet changing human needs; and one of the best things about them is that, in spite of themselves, they cannot remain as they are.

The envenomed controversy also as to which is the true theology, which for centuries has kept Christianity, in general, and Protestantism, in particular, fighting mad, seems largely futile, not because the discovery of the truth about God is unimportant, but because the idea that anybody has so discovered and defined God that he should controversially desire to enforce his opinion on another is absurd. All theology tentatively phrases in current thought and language the best that, up to date, thinkers on religion have achieved; and the most hopeful thing about any system of theology is that it will not last.

This does not mean that we are indifferentists about the church and skeptics about philosophy. To belittle the organization of religion will not do. As a bad trellis can ruin a good vine, or a poor government bedevil a civic community, so ecclesiastical institutions can either work havoc with religion or give it support and opportunity. As for doctrine, that always is important. Let a physician get his doctrine about scarlet fever right or he will bungle his task. So in religion we want the best churches and the truest thinking we can get. There are some kinds of theology and ecclesiastical practice in which most certainly we do not believe, and some kinds that seem to us wise, useful, and true. But religion is deeper than these. It created these in the first place, and it will persist long after their present forms have passed. Religion, therefore, cannot be essentially described in terms of its temporary clothes, its churches, and its creeds. Religion at its fountainhead is an individual, psychological experience.

III

Between religion conceived primarily in terms of churches and theologies and religion conceived primarily. as a psychological experience, at least one distinction is apparent. Churches and theologies can be inherited; from generation to generation they can be handed on, their doctrines written in books and their institutions passed from the custody of fathers to the custody of sons. Almost inevitably, therefore, churches and theologies become in time objects which believing people try to preserve. How much contemporary religion consists in the earnest, sometimes militant, frequently desperate, endeavor to save the churches and their theologies!

When, however, religion is looked at and sought for primarily as an individual, psychological experience, it at once becomes not so much something which the possessor must save as something which saves him. This distinction is fundamental. We may have a religion toward which the preservative attitude prevails, as though our supreme concern were somehow to save it, or we may have a religion which we do not worry much about saving, because it so vitally and visibly saves us.

Multitudes of people to-day are trying to preserve the organizations and thought-forms of religion. They are habitual steadiers of the Ark. Often with feverish militancy, always with deadly earnestness, they have made up their minds that religion must be saved. Such an attitude is a sure sign of religion's senility; it has uniformly preceded the downfall of those historic faiths that have grown old and passed away. In a religion's vigorous youth its devotees are not anxious about saving it, because it so powerfully saves them. And this is true because a young religion is not yet a static church or a settled theology to be preserved, but a psychological experience to be enjoyed.

This difference between a youthful and a senescent faith is evident in Christianity. While the early Christians battled stoutly for the things they believed, their major stress was not somehow to save their faith, anxiously defend it, and see it through. Their faith saved them, defended them, and saw them through. It carried them. It was to them health, peace, joy, and moral power. And whenever men thus have a religion which vitally saves them they have a religion which they need not worry much about saving.

The difference to-day between prevalent attitudes toward science on the one side and religion on the other ought to give us serious pause. Nobody solicitously is trying to save science for the simple reason that in its own sphere science is saving us. That is to say, it saves us from taking a covered wagon to San Francisco when we wish to consult a friend—we can use a telephone. It saves us from being isolated at sea—we can keep in touch with the whole world by radio. It may even save us from bothering about the sea at all when we go to Europe through the air. From many a disease, disability, and fear, science is positively saving us; and so long as science can go on saving us scientists need not worry much about saving it. Science is not yet primarily an organization to be maintained or a final creed to be preserved; it is still in the creative vigor of individual venturesomeness and exploration.

Turn, however, to religion! Read the books! Listen to the sermons! Multitudes of people are out with props trying to shore up religion. Theology endeavors it with new arguments; religious rotarians with new methods of salesmanship; practical ecclesiastics with new policies and programs, until the impression widely prevails that the major business of churchmen is somehow to keep religion going. That, however, was not the way Christianity started. The impression those first Christians made was that religion kept them going. So a religion that once was young and saved people now becomes old and has to be saved.

The school of thought which this book represents has no interest in this senile attitude. Our real task is to achieve a religion which saves people; and such religion must be primarily an individual, psychological experience.

We defend religion too much. Vital religion, like good music, needs not defense but rendition. A wrangling controversy in support of religion is precisely as if the members of an orchestra should beat folk over the head with their violins to prove that music is beautiful. But such procedure is no way to prove that music is beautiful. Play it! That, however, is a matter of spiritual creativity resident primarily in individuals.

IV

The content of such a creative religious experience as we have in mind is not easily described. If it takes various folk from Havelock Ellis to Saint John to make plain what love is, anything that one man writes about religion will surely be segmental. We may note, however, that whenever one finds people enjoying a religion which they do not worry about saving, because it saves them, there are two aspects to their experience, one active, the other receptive.

The gist of the active aspect lies in a basic fact: life faces us not only with things which give themselves to us and serve our interests but also with things to which we should give ourselves and which we should serve. Some elements in life are our slaves. We harness, bridle, and drive them. They are our hewers of wood and drawers of water. But so far is this from being the whole of life, it is not even the principal part.

In this scientific age when we commonly command law-abiding forces to our practical advantage, we are tempted to suppose that life's glory lies in the things which we master. The fact is, however, that our greatest hours never are associated with the things which we master but with the things which master us. Let a man compare the time when he learned to drive an automobile and felt the thrill of command over harnessed energy, with the day he first heard Beethoven's Fifth Symphony and was carried out of himself by something greater than himself, to which he gave himself!

Whenever anybody thus finds any goodness, truth, or beauty concerning which he feels not that it should give itself to him, but that he should give himself to it and be its loyal servant, that man has entered into an authentic religious experience.

That this approach to the meaning of religion is radically different from the common conventions of the churches is obvious. Here, for example, is a youth in straits about his religion. He has been reared in an inherited faith. It has consisted largely of a regimented system of religious opinions. He was drilled in them and consented to them as naturally as he consented to the fashion of his clothes or the articulation of his speech. Now, however, he has come to a university center. He is surrounded by new ways of thinking and fresh methods of dealing with knowledge. His religion begins perilously to disintegrate. At first he desperately tries to defend it, but it falls to pieces. For a long while he clings to the shreds, but now even these have gone. He has lost his religion.

The first thing to be said is that any religion which can be lost like that had something deeply the matter with it from the start, and that the youth would better not worry too much about losing it. What he would better do is to forget, at least for the time being, religion theologically defined and ecclesiastically organized, and go within himself to discover what religion means as a psychological experience. What if that youth, having lost an external and inherited religion, should discover that he is himself incurably religious and so come through to a religion which he will not need to defend, because it defends him, or laboriously carry, because it carries him, no longer weight to him but wings!

Try, then, saying to such a youth, "Your religion lost! Nothing more to live for!" Only recently a fine young fellow, in precisely this situation which I have described, came swiftly back at me when I spoke to him like that. "Nothing to live for?" he said in effect. "Upon the contrary, plenty to live for! Life is rich in things to give oneself to, truth to be discovered, beauty to create, social causes to serve, friendship to claim one's loyalty. I am in love with life because there is so much to be devoted to."

Obviously that youth had not lost religion. There

at the center of his real life he was being carried out of himself by something greater than himself to which he gave himself; only he did not recognize that wherever anyone thus finds any worthy thing concerning which he does not ask that it give itself to him but that he may give himself to it, he has discovered a genuine religious experience. It may not yet have achieved an adequate formulation; it may need clarification and development; but so far as it goes it is authentic religion and, because it is part and parcel of the man, not appended to him or merely inherited by him but spontaneously in him and an integral portion of him, it is often more vital and morally dynamic than any conventionally formulated stuff.

Doctor Noguchi, for example, is one of our modern martyrs in science. He isolated the germ of South American yellow fever and discovered the serum that would cure it. But the South American serum would not work in Africa. Some hidden differentiation eluded the investigators. So, against the protests of his colleagues, Doctor Noguchi went to the fever belt of Africa. It was his business, he said, and he was going to the heart of it. There, as his colleagues feared, he caught the disease, used the opportunity to experiment with his own blood, and finally died. He had found his loyalty and with re-joicing self-abnegation had given himself to it.

What Doctor Noguchi's formal religion was, if he had any, I do not know. But whatever it may have been, a life which thus had discovered its true meaning in self-committal to the more-than-self was in so far genuinely religious.

This approach to the meaning of religion is characteristic of many schools of thought to-day. Some put the matter one way, some another, but the diversity of expression only emphasizes the unity of intent.

Some say that the essence of religion is the sense of sacredness. Even the most carnal and insensitive mind must sometime have proved its human quality by feeling the presence of something sacred that ought not to be desecrated. Those things in human history of which the race has most reason to be proud spring from this sense of sacredness at its best. Truth for the scientist is sacred—to violate it is the unpardonable sin. Beauty to the artist is sacred—to wrong it is blasphemy. The rights of personality are to the man of moral insight sacred, and our economic exploitations are sacrilege. Why should man have emerged into this strange, compelling sense of the "holy," possessing rights over us so imperative that at our best we find our glory in serving it to the death? Huxley, the agnostic, flailed conventional religion but provided no substitute. Now his grandson, also eminent in science, rediscovers religion. "It is a way of life," he says, "which follows necessarily from a man holding certain things in reverence, from his feeling and believing them to be sacred."

This, however, is only putting into other words what we have just been saying. The sacred elements in life are those concerning which we feel, not so much that they belong to us as that we belong to them. They are not our servants, but we theirs. They have a right to our utter loyalty, and we find life's true meaning in giving it.

Others say that the essence of religion is worship. We truly live, they insist, not by virtue of those things that are beneath us but by virtue of those things that are above us. Our appreciations, admirations, and worships liberate life and give it worth. We spiritually are freed, not by what we enslave and use, but by what we adore. Therefore, the practical mastery over nature's law-abiding forces, which science confers, never can solve our human problem in its depths. Not what we command but what commands us determines destiny. The things we look down upon and merely utilize are less influential than the things we look up to and adore.

Religion so considered is essentially worship, and many a modern mind is rediscovering this central meaning of the worshiper's attitude. "Worship is the only possible way," says Professor Wieman, "to form those most subtle and complex habits of the heart and mind which organize and mobilize the total personality. . . . there is no other form of human endeavor by which so much can be accomplished." This approach to religion obviously agrees with what we have been saying, that religion is essentially the release of life through its committal to the highest that we know.

Professor Royce of Harvard used to express this truth in terms of loyalty. That to him was the center and soul of religion. Whoever finds his loyalty, so that life means not grasping what the self can get but giving to some worthy end what the self can expend, has found an authentic religious experience.

Such in our day is a characteristic approach to religion's meaning. It is primarily concerned not with formal creed and church but with inner experience. It should go without saying that from such individual experience of devotion to spiritual values comes the most sustained, tireless, and dependable service for social causes that the world knows.

V

Alongside this attitude of active self-committal, a receptive aspect is always present in a vitally saving faith. Inward communion from which come peace and power is characteristic of genuine religion. No one who has followed the work of religious psychology from William James to Starbuck and Coe will doubt the reality of such experiences. They are not matters of faith but of fact. They do actually occur. Phenomena such as conversion, transformation of character, and integration of personality through prayer can be studied objectively; and while some may think it possible to explain them on non-religious grounds no one thinks it possible to explain them away.

Indeed, a great deal of the unconventional religion of our day that has broken free from the orthodox churches is motivated mainly by a desire to recover religion as a resource of power, health, peace, and vitality in daily life. The explanation of the rise of cults like Christian Science and New Thought is obvious. While the old-line churches were largely concerning themselves with dogma, ritual, and organization, multitudes of folk were starving for available spiritual power with which to live. These cults arose to meet this need; and with all their mistaken attitudes toward scientific medicine, and their metaphysics, that to some of us is quite incredible, they have genuinely served millions of people by translating religion into terms of power available for daily use.

The preachers would better spare the breath they use in assailing such cults. What the Irishman said about the Socialists—"The only way to beat them is to beat them to it"—can be said also of these vitalistic movements in religion.

Indeed, here lies one of the major reasons why many youths to-day, weaned away from orthodox religion, if ever they were suckled on it, still know that religion itself is real. A typical young woman from the university, reared out of touch with organized Christianity and untrained in dogmatic faith, sought membership in the church. I wondered what the religion of this highly intelligent and unconventional young person was like, and was interested to discover that it consisted almost exclusively in the practice of affirmative prayer. That is, prayer did not mean to her reminding an individual called God to do something he had forgotten or urging him to bestow a blessing that otherwise he would not have been good enough to give. Prayer meant fulfilling inward conditions of attitude and receptivity and getting appropriate results in heightened insight, stability, peace, and self-control. Prayer was not magic, but the meeting of real conditions in a law-abiding, spiritual world and getting real results.

When religion means such commerce of the spirit it becomes as indispensable as food and drink. It is the vital center from which life's energies proceed. The possessor of this secret does not live from the teeth out, but taps resources of power that seem at least, as William James put it, to come up through the subconscious into consciousness from origins that are cosmic and not merely individual.

Such an experience secures power for daily living not by struggling after it but by inwardly releasing it. So driving a horse may be hard work, driving a spirited team very strenuous indeed, and handling a tally-ho and six an absorbing expenditure of energy. There is, however, a small room near Niagara Falls where a man sits quietly, speaks quietly, and at times walks quietly from dial to dial, but he is controlling five hundred thousand horse-power. When one knows how to do it, it is easier to release five hundred thousand horse-power than it is to drive one horse. Such is the secret of the spiritual adepts. They have achieved, not by the method of hard driving, but by the release of interior power adequate for life.

This experience is of the very essence of religion.

It substitutes confidence for fear, a sense of security for a life lived on the ragged edge; it takes people who thought they had to lift twenty pounds with only strength enough to lift ten, and transforms them into people who tackle life as a ten-pound load with strength to handle twenty. It inevitably affects health. Said one of the world's most famous psychologists to a friend of mine, "For complete psychological health mankind requires, either a religion, or some substitute for Religion which has not yet been discovered." Certainly this experience makes a difference to the integration of personality, to the moral drive of character, and to the radiance, tranquillity, hopefulness, and power with which men live.

VI

Take such a truncated description of personal religion for what it is worth! Let it stand as merely an indication of the major fact that multiplying numbers of people, when they think of religion, mean not a church, nor a system of theology, but a saving experience of inner spiritual devotion and daily spiritual power!

If the reader is impressed by the vagueness of all this, its disembodied churchlessness and its intellectual vacuity, lacking often the bones of idea and, therefore, likely to go flabby and impotent, he doubtless is right. To try to have "experience," like a homeless waif, abstracted from intellectual setting and unincorporated in a social group, is to endeavor the impossible.

That, however, is the very nub of the theological and ecclesiastical problem as the school of thought from which this book comes apprehends it. The present churches and the present theologies have too little to do with this saving experience of genuine spiritual devotion and daily spiritual power. Upon the contrary, a great deal of this vital religious experience has already fled from the churches and shaken off the dust of orthodoxy in order to get air to breathe and room to move about in. What have the differences between Baptists, Methodists, Presbyterians, and Episcopalians to do with such an experience of religion as we have been describing? Moreover, when the modern mind hears the creeds upon which many of the churches still insist, with all the corollaries brought out by controversy and urged as indispensables of religious truth—old cosmologies, doctrines of Biblical infallibility, miracles like virgin birth or physical resurrection—the reaction is not simply incredulity, although incredulity is undoubtedly emphatic—but wonder as to what such things have to do with religion.

As things are now, we cannot gather an ecumenical conference of Christians on church union without having three questions at once walk up stage as major matters of concern: the correct definition of the sacraments, the correct phrasing of ancient dogmas, the correct understanding of apostolic succession—before all of which an increasing number of religious people stand marveling that such things are supposed to be of interest to religion.

What we are driving at, therefore, is not what one writer scornfully calls "gossamer platitudes about the distinction between dogma and experience." We are insisting, rather, that the sort of dogma now enjoying ecclesiastical ascendency has no vital relation with the best spiritual life of our time, and that the sort of churches now existent are often stifling the life out of real religion.

As a matter of fact, we are deeply interested in theology. So far from thinking, for example, that non-theistic humanism is right in supposing that religion, being basically a psychological experience, can get on without God, many of us are vigorous contenders for the opposite. Moreover, we find God very near at hand and visibly operative. Consider the experience, whose individual aspects we have been discussing—a life carried out of itself by something greater than itself, to which it gives itself.

Such experience is not merely individual; it is racial. Something greater than humanity has laid hold upon humanity.

Richard Wagner wrote once to a friend, "If there were such a thing as a will capable of overruling the necessity of one's own being, I should assuredly will *not* to be an artist any longer. . . . Unhappily, though, there is no way of escape for me, and anything I could do to flee from art would be more artificial than art itself." Here was a man committed in spite of himself to something greater than himself, which commanded him as the necessity of his own being. That same thing has been true of humanity as a whole.

From our apelike progenitors in the forest we have come to our modern era of international hopes and, as the stars count time, we have done it in a few ticks of the astral clock. To say that we did it of ourselves is nonsense. It was the necessity of our being, as art was the necessity of Wagner's. Something in the marrow of the cosmic life from which we came laid this necessity upon us. We have been under a drastic mastery greater than our own. Looked at in the large, man, with his stupidities, his cruelties, his wanton frivolities and wars, appears across the ages desperately struggling to escape from an imperious necessity which will not

let him go. That necessity has lifted us up from the
ape-man to the present day, although no ape-man
ever dreamed of planning such a consequence. It has
swung us up the long spiral of human ascent, bringing us ever back to old problems, but forcing us
to face them upon higher levels, and driving us out,
whether we would or not, to larger co-operations and
more inclusive human fellowships. At times one
can fairly see man digging in his heels as though
resolutely refusing to go on. Something stronger
than humanity—call it what you will, necessity, fate,
God—has laid hold on humanity and will not loose
its grasp.

To be sure, even the leaders of the race have
often been tempted to discouragement. Man has
given them hemlock to drink, crucified them,
burned them at the stake. But always the falling
torch has been caught by another hand, and somehow the light has gone on. Wagner in the relentless grip of his art did not more truly face the necessity of his own being than humanity as a whole has
faced it.

Moreover, having with infinite cost come so far
from the Neanderthal man to modern society, from
stone-age huts to Chartres Cathedral, from primitive
tom-toms to Beethoven, from the savage right of
tooth and claw to the outlawry of war, we know well

that, no matter what the cost, we must keep on going. No more than Wagner can we "will *not* to be an artist any longer." Something stronger than mankind has laid hold upon mankind.

Squirm and twist as we will, we cannot be rid of this experiential fact which, of old, theologians phrased as the sovereignty of God, and which a poet like Francis Thompson calls the Hound of Heaven.

The materialists in all their various degrees and kinds are forced to attempt the explanation of this fact as due to the fortuitous organization of matter. But that, as an explanation, means nothing. For matter, to which has thus been ascribed the potency to become love and beauty, truth and honor, creative science and human brotherhood, is no longer matter at all but something else. All materialism labors under this fatal disability, that in order to get the actual human world explained as a material creation, it must endow matter with such potencies as make it no longer matter but a spiritual force gifted with the attributes of God.

If, then, materialism cannot even be materialistic without conferring on matter spiritual powers necessary to do what actually has been done, we need not be hesitant about using the word God. Indeed, it is precisely this factual and realistic approach to the idea of God which is characteristic of our time.

Less and less do we want a God who is merely a matter of faith. More and more we want a God who is a matter of fact.

Of this demand in present-day theology, men like Professor Whitehead of Harvard and Professor Wieman of Chicago are typical. Wieman is weary of the conventional God of "sugar and spice and all things nice." He understands, as any psychologist must, that the too comfortable God of our saccharine hymns is not real but a "defense mechanism" by which weak souls ward off disturbing contacts with this vast and often ruthless universe. But thus to perceive the falseness and futility of current ideas of God is not to have done with God. One of our most radical college presidents has lately said that the word "atheism" has passed from the vocabulary of the intelligent, and the real question now is, How shall we frame a true concept of God?

Such a concept must indubitably stop, as David Starr Jordan says about science, "where the facts stop," or thereabouts. But if this narrows its boundaries it also increases its reality. There is a Creative Factor in this universe favorable to personality, or else personality never would have arrived. A Cosmic Power is operative here, propitious to enlarging truth, creative beauty, and expanding goodness, or else they never would have existed. If by the term

God one means this, then one does most certainly mean something real and efficient in this universe whereof the picture-thinking of our religious symbolism is only the partial representative.

Some such confidence in God as this, to-day as always, is characteristic of religion. From Lotze and Höffding on, the interpretation of religion as faith in the conservation of life's spiritual values has been powerfully influential. Indeed, this would better be included in our description of religion as a psychological experience. Such experience begins with devotion to spiritual values; it goes on to confidence in their Conserver; it issues in such communion with him as brings peace and power.

VII

One immediate effect of such an approach to religious experience as we have been describing is to make its possessor sympathetic and tolerant. Within the framework of many creeds and rituals the inner realities of this experience thrive and grow; and one who cares primarily about the reality is generous toward its diverse and often incongruous settings. In a Buddhist temple I have heard a Japanese peasant praying with passionate devotion to Amida; in a Mohammedan mosque I have worshiped with a vast throng who bowed toward Mecca; at Assisi I

have knelt long at the tomb of St. Francis; and in more than one Protestant church, with sermons and hymns representing ways of thinking almost as strange to me as the worship of the Aztecs, I have found God. The very fact that one cares most about genuine devotion to moral values, confidence in their Conserver, and personal communion that brings peace and power, makes one sensitive to the presence of these factors in all sorts of places, and generous toward all environments that may contain them.

On shipboard we say "eight bells," on land, "twelve o'clock"; but if a man is interested in the essential matter he will not feel quarrelsome about the difference in terminology. So the approach to religion as a psychological experience undercuts ecclesiastical and theological diversities and makes its possessor at home in many religious settings from which otherwise his opinions would banish him.

Nevertheless, while the true possessor of this approach will be irenic and tolerant, he cannot be blind to the revolution that is involved in his major emphasis. When one thinks of the present churches, the lines along which they are divided, and the theological doctrines on which many of them still insist, it is clear that our existent ecclesiastical establishments are in their effect largely alien to, and sometimes in deadly conflict with, this inner meaning of

religion. They are insisting on things that do not matter to it. Their major emphases, controversies, rituals, and customs often draw attention away from it until one is not surprised to find some of the best religion of our time leaving the churches altogether and regarding them as hostile rather than friendly toward vital, spiritual life. Homiletical assault upon this attitude will do no good. This attitude has too much solid ground beneath it.

I expect no sudden revolution—history does not usually turn sharp corners. Dogmatic authoritativeness meets the need of confiding and unadventurous human nature too well to peter out soon. Denominationalism, although lacking a leg to stand on so far as common sense or serious care for the Kingdom of God is concerned, has too many strong loyalties associated with it to topple speedily. But if religion essentially is what we have said, then it cannot permanently be encumbered with the irrelevant sectarianism and antagonistic world-views of many of our contemporary churches.

Meanwhile, some of us, so far from deserting the churches, have redoubled our devotion, like citizens who choose difficult days as the time when it most is necessary not to despair of the republic. We will not reduce ourselves to any denomination's lowest common denominator; we will not put our

necks into the yoke of any official creed; we will try
to see straight and say honestly what we see. To call
young men of this spirit to the ministry, as though
to be a Christian preacher meant not to enter a conventional profession but to undertake an adventurous prophethood, is the great desideratum. The need
of the churches is leadership.

The tragedy of religion to-day is that multitudes,
hungry amid the conventionalities of our ecclesiasti-
cism, are wandering homeless, like Kipling's cat "by
his wild lone." Wanting religion as a saving experience, one sees them on all sides getting help by
nibbles, lacking intellectual articulation for their
thought or any sense of human companionship in
seeking what they desire. They want spiritual homes
to which they can belong. They want intellectual
justification for a sustaining faith. And up through
all this uncertain welter come at times sure signs of
bona fide religion—folk within the churches and
outside them who know what is meant by genuine
spiritual devotion, confidence in the Conserver of
life's spiritual values, and communion with him that
brings peace and power.

The one thing that backward, sectarian, and ob-
scurantist churches need most to fear is such religion.
They need not in the least fear the attacks of the
irreligious. Religion can whip irreligion on any field

at any time. But from the days of Buddha in India and Christ in the Roman Empire, an aged and decrepit religion clinging to its crutches has always needed to fear a youthful movement of the spirit, a vigorous and spontaneous emergence of religious experience in its essential meanings.

The only thing that ever yet has been able to reform religion is religion.

What Is Christianity?

THE first work of intellect is discrimination, and nowhere in the field of religion is that more needed than in comparing with one another the great faiths of mankind. The older attitude of Christians was to call their own religion true and to lump under "heathendom" man's other worships and beliefs. Missionary maps printed the so-called Christian portions of the planet white while the remainder was indiscriminately black. To state the matter with restraint, this idea is no longer tenable.

Indeed, to many it has become so patently absurd that, in reaction against it, they now conceive all religions to be indifferently of one quality. Hinduism, Buddhism, Jainism, Zoroastrianism, Bahaism, Judaism, Christianity—all these, we are told, spring from the same spirit and at heart mean one thing. At inter-religious conferences sweeping assertions are made that the prophets and founders of the world's religions all "speak the same language" and "strike the same note." Irenic and polite though this is, it happens not to be true.

Moreover, this sentimental reduction of mankind's faiths to such a minimum that unity can somehow be wangled out of them does no honor to the faiths themselves. If I were a Buddhist I should not wish to be told that Buddhism is identical with Christianity. Buddhism has profound and distinctive sources and has pursued a historic course of development rich in peculiar associations and meanings; to lose these differential elements in religious abstractions which can be indifferently affirmed of all faiths does Buddhism no honor. The glory of a religion lies in its unique contributions.

While, therefore, every liberal mind desires a growing *rapprochement* among the world's faiths, the wise will not try to achieve it by loosely asserting an identity which does not exist. By appreciating, rather than by forgetting, the characteristic elements of each religion we are most likely to achieve fraternity.

What, then, is Christianity?

Starting in Galilee nearly two thousand years ago, it has run an amazing course. Diverse ages, races, and temperaments have played upon it. In it can be found all the dominant types of religious experience and expression known to mankind. Upon it mystics, metaphysicians, and moralists of many sorts have left their mark. It has become stark asceticism in some, and in others it has assumed the pomp of ecclesiastical autocracy. It has been pacifist in the Quaker, and militarist in the Crusader. It includes within its historic movement many kinds of theology, from the frontiers of pantheism to the borders of polytheism, and many sorts of sacramental theory from magic up. What is Christianity? The more one knows about it, the more difficult the answer becomes.

To many a youth this is no merely theoretical inquiry. He has always supposed himself a Christian but now he is bewildered as to what being a Christian means. He may sit in a classroom with a Buddhist on one side and a Confucianist on the other. Sometimes he understands them better than he understands certain types of Christians to whose talk in chapel he must listen. Christianity no longer is the simple thing it used to seem to him. Apparently it can mean almost anything. He hears a preacher say that it is like a snowball which has rolled across the centuries and picked up *en route* all sorts of refuse and débris.

Yet it must be possible to get some clarity about this matter. There must be some quality that specially characterizes the Christian philosophy of life and constitutes its major contribution to the world. What, then, is Christianity?

II

Whatever differential factors may characterize the Christian religion, they certainly are not discoverable where popular orthodoxy commonly looks for them. All the superficial elements of orthodox Christianity can, I think, be paralleled in non-Christian faiths. Acceptance of an inspired Book is no peculiarity of Christians. In the theories which Islam holds about the Koran, or Hinduism about the Rig Veda, in the uses to which these holy books have been put, and in the methods of interpretation employed upon them, one finds reduplicated all the characteristic ideas and practices associated with the Bible.

Miracles are certainly no specialty of Christian faith. They are the psychological children of the ancient world-view, and while dressed in diverse clothes, Indian, Chinese, Japanese, or Palestinian, they are recognizably akin. The same kind of miracle, such as raising the dead, transforming one element, like water, into another, walking on the sea, and feeding multitudes with a small food supply, is found familiarly among the records of historic faiths.

The deification and worship of the religion's founder is no peculiarity of Christianity, nor is the ascription to him of a miraculous birth. Indeed, that latter idea not only appears in one form or another with reference to Buddha, Zoroaster, Lao-tse, and Mahavira, but is used as a common explanation of extraordinary personality in cases that lie outside religion proper, like Augustus Cæsar. Whether appearing in forms gross or refined, its commonness makes evident how familiar an idea it used to be in accounting for outstanding people. Origen, the Christian apologist of the third century, when pleading for the Virgin Birth of Jesus, took this fact for granted. "According to the Greeks themselves," he wrote, "all men were not born of a man and woman. . . . There is no absurdity in employing Grecian histories to answer Greeks, with a view of showing that we are not the only persons who have recourse to miraculous narratives of this kind. For some have thought fit, not in regard to ancient and heroic narratives, but in regard to events of very recent occurrence, to relate as a possible thing that Plato was the son of Amphictione . . . by Apollo." Justin Martyr, born not long after the composition of the synoptic gospels, put it more bluntly. "If we even affirm that He was born of a virgin, accept this in common with what you accept of Perseus."

Since the disaster of the Great War, and the consequent discouragement about the world's fu-

ture, we have had a recrudescence of premillennial-
ism; and Fundamentalists have been insisting on the
second coming of Christ as a necessary item of
Christian faith. They are certainly nearer right than
some liberals are on one point: very probably Jesus,
and most assuredly his first disciples, did expect just
such a sudden ending of the age and cataclysmic coming of the Kingdom as the premillennialists predict.
This belief, however, is not at all peculiar to Christians. The Mohammedan expectation of the returning Mahdi comes from the same psychological
sources; and the Shi'ah of Persia still are awaiting
the return of Muhammad, son of Hasan al-Askari,
who has been about to appear since the third Islamic
century. As for Buddhists, they are expecting
Maitreya, the next Buddha. Already in the Tusita
heaven he is awaiting the divine moment to descend
to earth and restore the Law. The imaginative hopes
of his epiphany are cut from the same pattern as the
Messianic expectations of the Hebrews, and, "Oh,
that I might live to see Allenya Metai!" is the earnest prayer of many Buddhist hearts.

No matter where one looks in Christianity one
finds in its ostentatious orthodoxies, in the items of
faith and practice pushed to the front by its controversies and commonly insisted on as indispensable
to its integrity, elements entirely familiar to the

students of non-Christian faiths. Various religions exhibit similar doctrines and practices with reference to the sacraments; ideas associated with atonement are present in all highly developed faiths; "No one can be saved without regeneration" sounds Christian, but is a quotation from a non-Christian, Greco-Roman Mystery Religion; and even justification by faith, so far from being exclusively Pauline or Lutheran, is being stated to-day and lived upon with peace and joy by one of the powerful Buddhist sects. As for customs such as pilgrimage, relic-worship, and the like, they appear everywhere. One who has seen Christians, Mohammedans, and Hindus on pilgrimage cannot mistake the common psychological elements in their behavior; while between the bones of the Three Wise Men in Cologne Cathedral and the holy tooth of Buddha in Ceylon there are differences of historic detail but none of essential meaning.

When one plunges deeper and thinks of vital matters, such as prayer and philanthropic love, Christianity has no monopoly. If Jesus said, "When thou prayest, enter into thine inner chamber, and having shut thy door, pray to thy Father who is in secret," Epictetus said, "When you have shut your doors, and darkened your room, remember never to say that you are alone; for you are not alone, but God is within." If the Christian scriptures say, "Love your enemies, and do them good, and lend," the Buddhist scriptures say, "By calmness let a man overcome wrath; let him overcome evil by good; the miser let him subdue by liberality, and the liar by truth."

No longer are these resemblances explicable in terms of borrowing, nor is it possible to say, with the early Catholic missionaries in Mexico and Peru, that the devil to frustrate them had forehandedly furnished the people with a caricature of Christianity. These widespread and deep-seated resemblances between separated faiths, beginning in primitive religion, as all readers of Frazer's *Golden Bough* know, and running up into the highly organized religions, have psychological explanations; they are due, not to mutual copying, but to similar emotional reactions to the mystery of the world and the deep needs of human nature.

The days are gone when wise adherents of Christianity are jealous of this world-wide dissemination of common ideas. One should as soon feel jealousy because architectural beauty is to be found in the Taj Mahal and not exclusively in Gothic cathedrals, as to envy Buddhism its spirit of love, or regret that Islam teaches men to pray. Indeed, the universality of an idea or practice is a weighty evidence of its working power; and the prevalence of even such conceptions as Christian orthodoxy shares with other faiths shows the deep-seated human needs to which they have ministered.

Nevertheless, the combination of these similar elements in the various faiths brings widely different results. White paper and black coal may both be carbon compounds, but, for all that, they are unmistakably diverse in nature and function. So Buddha and Christ do not on the whole speak the same language nor strike the same note. Their followers have a difficult time understanding one another. The various religions are really various, and the study of their distinctive elements is at least as important as emphasis upon their unities.

In what terms, then, can we describe that quality which gives peculiar flavor to Christianity so that when it is absent Christianity is not Christian at all? This differential seems to reside in one major matter, discoverable elsewhere, to be sure, but so emphatic in Christianity, so dominant in the Founder's message, so unescapable in the ethic of the movement which succeeded him, that from it as from a fountain flows the result which makes Christianity Christian.

The genius of Christianity lies in reverence for personality.

III

At first sight, this reduction of the manifold complex called the Christian religion to so simple a formula will seem to many the substitution of a thin abstraction for a rich reality. But this abstraction is not thin; like Aladdin's lamp, it has amazing potencies which have built into the Christian system its distinctive and abiding qualities.

Were one to select the special contribution which Jesus of Nazareth himself has made and is making to man's thought, one could do no better than to call him the champion of personality. Some have tried reducing Jesus to a poetic dreamer who loved flowers and children and held beautiful but impractical ideals. Renan, for example, says, "Tenderness of heart was in him transformed into infinite sweetness, vague poetry, universal charm." That, however, so far from adequately representing the historic Jesus, bleaches the color all out of him.

Others have reduced Jesus to an ecclesiastical reformer who, rebelling against the shams of institutional religion, got himself crucified in consequence. Certainly he was an ecclesiastical reformer concerning whom the religious dignitaries of his time felt, as in Shaw's drama King Charles felt about Joan of Arc when he said, "If only she would keep quiet, or go home!" That, however, does not represent the initial motive of his ministry.

Others have represented Jesus as a social reformer, a prophet of the Kingdom of God, who foresaw a reign of righteousness and brotherhood on earth and willingly died for it. That picture of him undoubtedly is true, but his social prophethood was the consequence of something profound in his philosophy.

Others have thought chiefly of Jesus as a metaphysical hypostasis, the second person of the Trinity. Such theological endeavor to explain him in terms of philosophy current in the ancient Greek world was inevitable; but Jesus of Nazareth himself was something quite different from a metaphysical hypostasis. He was an historic character, making a concrete and describable contribution to human thought. He was the champion of personality. He laid hold on that, lifted it up, conceived it in all its appearances in child, woman, peasant, or king as infinitely valuable. Moreover, he thought of personality as the central fact in the universe and used it as the medium of interpretation for all other facts.

Seen against the background of the centuries which immediately preceded him this constitutes the uniqueness of Jesus' message. Whether one is a Christian or not does not primarily depend on the acceptance or rejection of the orthodoxies of official church and creed. Give new names to many of these creedal conceptions and ecclesiastical practices and one may be a Buddhist, or a Hindu, or a Mohammedan. Whether one really is a Christian or not depends on whether one accepts or rejects Jesus' attitude toward personality.

IV

During this next generation Christianity will probably have to fight for its life, and the struggle will concern itself more and more manifestly with this central matter. Rear-guard actions will continue around belated disputes about ancient miracles, Biblical infallibility, and what not; but the crux of the conflict will not be there. Can we in this modern world maintain Jesus' attitude toward personality? The answer to that question is the sign of a falling or rising Christianity.

If one thing more than another seems to fly in the face of appearances, it is the statement that personality is the primary and victorious element in this universe. Here we human persons are upon this revolving planet in the sky. We are very tiny, and the universe is huge. Our span of life is brief, while the universe was crashing on unimaginable ages before we were born and will crash on after we have departed. We are frailty itself, at the mercy of a few particles of disordered matter, so that a slight accident can snuff us out like guttering candles. Tenuous and temporary, a human being seems anything but triumphant in this overwhelming cosmos. Yet at its best Christianity has taken up the cudgels for personality, for its divine origin, spiritual nature, infinite worth, and endless possibilities.

Take it or leave it, that is what Christianity is about. That is its guiding star and its dynamic faith. Personality, the most valuable thing in the universe, revealing the real nature of the Creative Power and the ultimate meaning of creation, the only eternal element in a world of change, the one thing worth investing everything in, and in terms of service to which all else must be judged—that is the essential Christian creed. Like it or not, the Christian religion, to use James Harvey Robinson's phrase, is "heavily anthropocentric."

If anyone wishes to argue that the appearances are against this estimate of personality, I agree. The appearances are certainly against it—size, for example. Consider the star, Betelgeuse, which, brought nearer to the earth, would fill the entire horizon, and then try to assert the conviction that man, a mere pygmy, is the triumphant element here! The appearance of time is against it. In the vast cosmic cycles why should man, appearing yesterday, expect to last beyond to-morrow? The appearance of strength is against it, as anyone must feel who has experienced or even has imagined an earthquake shaking men to destruction, as a lion shakes off vermin. As for death, that looks as though—like the magnetic rock in the old legend—it pulls all the nails from the timbers of our ships until they disintegrate in the deep. One who wishes to win the argument on the basis of appearance can have it.

I cannot, however, imagine anyone who has followed the course of science and philosophy being deeply impressed by so easy a winning. Appearances prove little or nothing. It certainly does not look as though our clear sense of up-and-down were pure illusion, and that half the time we are hanging by our heels on the underside of a revolving globe. It does not look as though solid steel were made of electrons operating by hundreds in atomic nuclei—each nucleus one ten-billionth of a pin point. As for the cosmos at large, which seems obvious enough, it surely does not look like Einstein's curved space-time.

The outstanding attribute of materialism is its naïveté. It bets on the appearances, while if anything seems certain, it is that the ultimate nature of reality must lie at least as much deeper than appearance as do the truths of astronomy, physics, and mathematics. It might conceivably be that not matter but personality constitutes the key to the truth.

Certainly, big as it is, the universe would have no meaning without personality. Some silent, swift catastrophe conceivably might blot out all mental and spiritual life. Nothing would be left except the universe minus personality. Planets would swing in their courses with no eye to see. Wind would blow in the trees and surf break on the rocks with no ear to hear. Sunrise and sunset would mark the revolution of the earth with none to care. Age after age the stars would shine with no mind to interpret. There would be no science to explain, poetry to praise, art to depict, music to celebrate, or character to give response—nothing but endless things without personality.

Even if one does not fully assent to them, one can understand those philosophies which assert that in large measure a universe like that would be not only meaningless but non-existent, since personalities, by their canons of interpretation and formulations of law, not only observe but help to create the very cosmos in which they live. What is color without an eye? What is the "law of gravitation" without a mind? Somehow an absolutely mindless universe simply is not a universe. Even physical science, when it gets back to the ultimate reality which it can glimpse behind molecules, atoms, electrons, and protons, finds a series of mathematical relationships. Now, mathematical relationships, whatever else they may be, are mental.

Moreover, the possibilities of creation seem to be locked up in personality. Look existence over and only here in this amazing thing—self-conscious being with powers of intellect, creative hope, and love— is there any promise of development; only in what this pregnant and potential being may yet become does the cosmos, so far as we can see, have any future.

Long before we faced this problem in our modern terms, Christ took up the cause of personality's pre-eminence. Like a true son of his time and people, he did not speak about it in abstract terms. He was concrete, picturesque, poetic, dramatic. He said that when one personality turned from spiritual failure to success all the angels sang; that it was not the Father's will that one personality, even in a child, should perish; that quality of character was revealed primarily in the way we treated personality in others; and that to gain the whole world was an unprofitable bargain if one failed in building personality within oneself.

If the essence of religion lies in the sense of

sacredness, then no doubt beclouds the nature of Jesus' religion. To him personality was supremely sacred. Mankind's faith for ages had dealt with holy rocks, mountains, trees, and caves, sacred temples, sacred days, sacred sacraments; the sense of holiness had attached itself to an endless variety of things, animals, customs, and personages. But Jesus cared for none of these. He allocated the sense of sacredness to one place—personality. Nothing on earth was sacred to him save as it contributed to personality some increment of what he called life more abundant. Whether he healed the body, taught the mind, or inspired the spirit, whether he attacked economic customs that exploited people, or risked his life against an ecclesiastical system that misguided them, he was motived by one central principle—the utter sacredness of personality.

That attitude constitutes the essence of Christianity. It is either magnificent or mad. It certainly is not tame.

Mr. H. L. Mencken, describing the desire of reforming Christians to recover the ethical principles of Jesus and try to live by them, says, "All this is grateful to my gills." I wonder! Mr. Mencken says that the cosmos is a gigantic flywheel making ten thousand revolutions a minute and that "man is a sick fly taking a dizzy ride on it." He calls man "a local disease of the cosmos—a kind of pestiferous eczema." He values man as "the supreme clown of creation, the *reductio ad absurdum* of animated nature." One suspects that Mr. Mencken would have more trouble with Jesus than with any other character in history, not at all because the Master would be guilty of those ministerial "wowserisms" that he so violently abhors, but because Jesus was the champion of personality and said his most scathing words, not against heretics, nor even against sinners, but against cynics.

The "simple Jesus" is not simple in the least. He is the leading representative among men of a tremendous philosophy of life. As Ralph Waldo Emerson put it, "Alone in all history he estimated the greatness of man."

V

That this Christian idea of personality has some hard sledding ahead of it seems clear. It runs into headlong collision with prevalent ideas: that man, for example, is a physical machine made by the fortuitous self-arrangement of matter, with interesting mental and spiritual by-products. An ingenious scientist has invented a mechanical dog with selenium eyes which, when one flashes a light into the eyeballs, will follow the glare about the room—an amazingly clever physicochemical machine. (Human personality is being so conceived; and our thinking, loving, creating are not uncommonly pictured as highly complicated chemical operations.)

To be sure, serious difficulties exist of which even the proponents of this view are conscious. If a human being is only a physical machine, he is at least a queer kind of physical machine, doing things that ordinarily machines are not supposed to do. For example, we aspire, setting our hearts on high ideals and striving after them. Imagine a machine doing that—a Ford car longing to be a Rolls-Royce. Moreover, we repent, sometimes wondering in agony whether, after tragic moral failure, it is possible to hope for pardon and recovery again. That experience does not seem identical with a chemical operation. Even on the physical plane we human machines generate little machines called children, that grow up from infancy to maturity. I forbear imagining the consequence if Ford cars should do that.

The behaviorists are right in insisting on the mechanistic aspects of the personal organism. Moreover, they are thereby making available an eminently useful method of investigation and control, with important consequences bound to come from it. When, however, they cease being scientists dealing with working hypotheses and try to become philosophers formulating dogmas, they fare no better than other dogmatists. They become enslaved to words. They call us machines, but we are obviously machines that think, love, distinguish between right and wrong, repent, follow ideals, sacrifice for one another, believe in God, hope for immortality, and construct philosophies to explain the universe. That is to say, we are not anything which anybody in his senses can mean by a machine.

The more insistent and dangerous enemies of the Christian philosophy, however, are not our fads of materialistic theory, but our abiding attitudes of moral selfishness. Wherever personality is being cramped, fettered, debilitated, and abused, there Christianity is being denied. If the churches would put that idea in the foreground of their minds they might get some Christian things done instead of remaining what too largely they are—societies for the propagation of an outgrown mythology.

It was on this moral side that Jesus approached the problem of personality. He came at the matter, as he came at all matters, not theoretically, but practically. He cared about people and believed in them. He leaped the barriers which caste and convention had erected and was in this sense the first great democrat. His major parables concern the treatment of persons. How the Good Samaritan dealt with the victim of the robbers, how the family handled the returning prodigal—such matters seemed to him so crucial that for him the (divine judgment was altogether concerned with the way people, especially the poor, the sick, and the imprisoned, had been treated.) Even the most sacred institutions, like the sabbath, and by implication all other forms of human society as well, are to be judged by their effect on people. They were made for man, not man for them.

This elevation of personality's value has produced in the Christian movement a certain militant and aggressive unwillingness to leave things as they are so long as people are being wronged. Say the worst you will about Christendom, it is, nevertheless, the place where democracy has had its best chance, where science has at last got under way, where education has been most freely given to children, where poverty has been most tirelessly attacked, where philanthropy has been practiced on the largest scale, and where to-day the general public conscience is most disturbed about industrial exploitation and war. To credit all this to Christianity would be incredible; but Christianity has been one of the major ingredients in the civilization where this has been true.

To be sure, the most anti-Christian attitudes have often controlled the churches. Many ecclesiastics have discouraged humanitarian movements, backed tyranny, defended slavery, blocked endeavors to improve industry, end child labor, and abolish war, and in general have been among the world's worst citizens. But always underneath such official religion that other element, without which no Christianity is ever Christian, has worked like leaven. In its nobler hours, Christianity has been unable to escape from the spirit of its Founder, and has known that its essential business in this world is the championship of personality.

VI

So far as the theory of Christian personalism is concerned, one of the major problems which the modern mind faces centers in the idea of God which is involved. For the Christian enthusiast for personality inevitably approaches God in personal terms.

Many to-day have desperate difficulty with this endeavor so to think of God as personal, and no wonder! The universe does not on the whole act as though it were under efficient personal supervision and control. When I hear some hymns, sermons, and prayers taking for granted or asserting with naïve simplicity that this vast, ruthless cosmos, with all the monstrous accidents which it involves, is a neatly planned and personally conducted tour, I recall the more reasonable hypothesis of an East African tribe.

"They say," reports an observer, "that although God is good and wishes good for everybody, unfortunately he has a half-witted brother who is always interfering with what he does." That, at least, bears some resemblance to the facts. God's half-witted brother might explain some of life's sickening and insane tragedies which the idea of an omnipotent individual of boundless good will toward every soul most certainly does not explain.

To be sure, we can use our wits to some effect in justifying the ways of God to man. There are four factors in creation from which come all human tragedy and pain. First, the law-abiding nature of the universe that will not vary its procedure to save anyone; second, the progressive nature of human life, that starting us with ignorance, disease, poverty, slavery, or war, makes us fight our way through difficulties and over obstacles to a better future; third, individual initiative and self-determination by whose misuse we often mess up our own lives and ruin others'; fourth, our intermeshing relationships, so unifying our fortunes that what happens to one of us always befalls others too.

From these four factors come all the calamities of men. Yet would we be willing to eliminate any of the four? Would we make the universe whimsical and not law-abiding, or make human life static and not progressive, or make ourselves automata with no initiative, or break up all human relationships and leave our lives isolated like bottles in the rain? All our calamities come from the same factors that provide our opportunities and joys; and were one of us granted omnipotence for an hour he might well hesitate, in spite of the suffering involved, to disturb this fourfold basis of the world.

Nevertheless, when our wits have done their best, life is still an abysmal mystery. Modern Christian thought frankly faces the fact that in our popular pictures of God as "a sort of infinitely magnified and improved Lord Shaftesbury," who creates, plans, supervises, and controls every event in the universe as an omnipotently affectionate and efficient individual might do if he had a free hand, we have added another idol to the list of man's theological images. Christian thought, however, insists that the recognition of this does not mean that we are thrown back on an impersonal idea of God as blind force, uninterested in man and his values as the weather is careless of the flowers.

All intelligent endeavor after an idea of God must begin its quest with reverent agnosticism, with the recognition that whatever we affirm about God can be only a partial and inadequate symbol. When a child begins to study geography he thinks of Italy as like a boot. So it is, but how inadequate a statement about the Italy of Michelangelo and Raphael, Petrarch and Dante, of Venice, Florence, and Rome! Whatever language we little children on this wandering island in the sky ever use about God is like that—a far-off, partial symbol. (We are picture-thinkers when we talk about God and we cannot help it, and our pictures, drawn from limited experience, cover only an infinitesimal fragment of the whole.)

To suppose that such acknowledgment of the incomprehensibility of God is skepticism is absurd. "All that can be said about God is *not* God, but only certain smallest fragments which fall from His table"—Saint Catherine of Genoa said that. "Divine things are not named by our intellect as they really are in themselves, for in that way it knows them not; but they are named in a way that is borrowed from created things"—Saint Thomas Aquinas himself said that. Nobody, I suspect, who has imagination enough to grasp the problem can think otherwise. What we can say about God to what is left unsaid is, as James Martineau remarked, "as the rain-drop to the firmament."

It is important, however, to say what we can say as truly as possible. Whether we take a mechanistic, physicochemical process as our picture of God, saying, as another put it, that the ultimate reality is a combination of phosphorus and glue, or whether we take personal life at its best as our admittedly inadequate endeavor to represent him in our thought and devotion, does make an immense difference. What Christianity is at this point admits of no doubt. It is once more the champion of personality. (It regards personal life as so significant in the universe that it can be used as the symbol in terms of which we think least inadequately about God.)

Accept it or reject it, Christianity involves that. It challenges every merely mechanistic interpretation of the world. It regards materialism as of all systems of magic the most incredible. For materialism is magic. To suppose that physical particles maneuvering in the void fortuitously arranged themselves into planets, forests, mothers, musicians, artists, poets, scientists, and saints is not to work out a philosophy; it is to run away from philosophy and believe in magic.

As for Christianity, its primary postulate is regulative for its idea of God. It discovers him most surely and significantly within personal life. When it is intelligent it does this modestly, taking in earnest Paul's assertion that "at present we only see the baffling reflections in a mirror." All its ideas of God are admittedly symbols, intimations, adumbrations, suggestions; they certainly are not definitions. It rejoices that we cannot comprehend God, for if we could he would not be worth comprehending. It does not suppose that we have achieved more than an infantile lisp when, with our delimited experience of personal life, we utter our profoundest assertions that God is personal. But it does everlastingly return to the proposition that personal life is the road out toward the truth.

The gist of what the church has meant by the Divinity of Jesus lies in the idea that, if God is to be symbolized by personal life, he should be symbolized by the best personal life we know. The interpretation of the Spiritual World in terms of personality and the interpretation of personality in terms of Christ—that is in brief the summary of Christian theology.

VII

Inevitably, this philosophy issues in the hope of immortality. If one tells a modern Christian that that hope is vain, that the survival of the personal organism after death is so against all known possibilities as to be incredible, the Christian, I suppose, might answer somewhat as follows:

Imagine twin babes, unborn in their mother's womb, gifted with the power of thought, the one a skeptic and the other a believer. They are living without light and without breathing, both of which would be to them unthinkable. The crisis of birth, tearing them loose from the matrix on which their existence seems fundamentally to depend, would appear to them like death. As for picturing the world without, that would be impossible.

The skeptic babe could say to the believer, "You are only a wishful thinker; you desire to go on living and so you think you will. How can you be decently scientific and think that? You see how absolutely our existence depends on present circumstances. You are credulous to suppose that the disruption of them will still leave us alive."

To which the believing babe could reply, "My faith is not mere wishful thinking. Month after month nature has been at work here developing something so marvelous that I am confident of an aftermath. Nature is not utterly irrational. She means something by all these preparations, and something will come of them."

To which the skeptic might retort, "How, then, do you picture the new life? If you are so sure about the future, describe it! What is it like?"

This would obviously put the believing babe in a difficult situation. "I do not know how to picture it," he would have to say. "It is to me unimaginable, but it may still be true. I am agnostic about all details. Only of this I feel confident, that nature is not so senseless as to undertake such a promising process with no end in view. The crisis that you call death will turn out really to be birth."

I sympathize deeply with that believing unborn babe. He is in the same case with multitudes of Christians. The outward appearances admittedly are against life after death. Nevertheless, not the skeptic babe but the believer would be right. The crisis did look like death but it was not. It was birth.

At any rate, Christianity, being the champion of personality, is irrevocably the religion of hope. It sees this world as a home for the rearing of persons, not as a gallows on which ultimately they will all be hanged.

Such is the essential genius of Christianity. Whether one looks at its morals, its metaphysics, or its characteristic emotional reactions, reverence for personality is the key to their understanding. In the preceding chapter we said that religion begins in devotion to spiritual values, is undergirded by confidence in their Conserver, and issues in communion that brings peace and power. When, however, one finds such psychological elements of religious experience in their typically Christian forms they are always shaped by personalism and colored by its hues. Spiritual values are conceived in terms of enrichment to personality; the Conserver is symbolized by personality at its best; the communion is with an unseen friend.

One does not mean that this emphasis is so exclusively Christian as to be undiscoverable in other faiths. That claim would be absurd. No faith would fail to assert that love for people as expressed in practical service is part and parcel of true religion. Listen to Buddha: "As a mother at the risk of her life watches over her own child, her only child, so also let everyone cultivate a boundless friendly mind towards all beings. And let him cultivate good will towards all the world, a boundless friendly mind, above and below and across, unobstructed, without hatred, without enmity. This (way of) living they say is the best in the world."

Yet I am confident that a Buddhist would at once acknowledge that the genius of his religion is far from identical with such enthusiasm for personality as this paper has described. Indeed, a good Buddhist might stoutly assert his satisfaction that his faith holds to another view altogether. Individual existence, he might say, is an illusion; we are like bubbles on the sea, and our peace is to be reabsorbed into its endlessly prolific depths. Continuance of individual existence, he might insist, is a curse; and only

Nirvana, with the quietude of a candle that has been blown out, is the ultimate hope.

Not all schools of Buddhist thought would say exactly that; they are as diverse as are the multitudinous sects of Christendom; but no one who knows the genius of Buddhism can possibly mistake it for Christianity. Even at the risk of seeming prejudiced, I think Buddhism is a defeatist philosophy. It despairs of personality, thinks it transient and futile, counsels the renunciation of desire as the remedy for ill, and in the meantime pities men that they must exist at all. Christianity is aggressive and spiritually militant. It believes in personality, its infinite possibility, its permanent continuance, its ultimate victory.

Meanwhile, multitudes of people in our so-called Christian land will find it exceedingly difficult in the next generation to be Christians. For some, behavioristic psychology and materialistic philosophy will make the Christian ideas of personal value seem untrue and, for others, the forces of commercial exploitation and selfish greed will make them seem unreal. Many will fall back on being Christians within limits, believing in the sacredness of personality, more or less. In their better moments they will dare to think high thoughts about it, but faith in man will prove too difficult to hold steadily, and God and immortality will seem too good to be true.

The fact is there never have been many Christians. There have been millions of believers in the pagan and semi-pagan accretions which ecclesiastical Christianity has held in common with other faiths, but Christians, who shared Jesus' reverence for personality, have been few and far between.

This is the real challenge to the churches.

What have their sectarian divisions to do with reverence for personality? What have their theological wrangles in common with the cause that Jesus of Nazareth had at heart? What if they could be made to see that their primary business is the championship of personality! What if the enrichment of personality by worship or by better schools, a juster economic system, and a warless world, could become their great enthusiasm! What if the philosophy involved in this championship, interpreting reality in terms of spiritual values instead of dirt, could absorb their thought! Such a perception of what Christianity is might cause as salutary a revolution as ever has convulsed and reconstructed the churches. It might even make Christianity Christian!

Religion Without God?

I N INTELLECTUAL importance the most considerable religious movement recently set afoot is non-theistic humanism. Self-conscious adherents may not as yet be numerous, but many of our "best minds" are plainly humanistic, the major positions of the movement accord with current thinking, and already various groups of avowed humanists are bidding for popular recognition and support.

It is regrettable that still another meaning has been added to an already protean word. In art and literature humanism has been a liberating force with a long and notable history. We may not charge the religious humanists to-day with being hermit crabs that have deliberately crawled into the protecting shell of an old term, but certainly the non-theistic humanitarianism for which they stand has little or no relationship with artistic and literary humanism past, present, or to come. Even in religious usage, humanism is a fluid term and in some of its meanings represents ideas to which any Christian could give hearty assent, but specifically the word is claimed by those who, like a recent exponent, say, "The belief in God and the belief in immortality are gone."

Such humanists—and it is with such only that this chapter deals—are sure of goodness, truth, and beauty; are confident that in the experience and creation of these spiritual values human life finds its distinctive meaning, and that in any sort of universe, theistic or materialistic, with God or without him, the center and circumference of human worth must lie in the personal exploration of these values and the creation of a society which incarnates them.

Evangelical preachers commonly draw forbidding pictures of life's Saharan waste when faith in God departs, but the humanists will have none of that. They not only give up God; the more jubilant of them are glad to be rid of him. At least they are sure that faith in God has had its dangerous disadvantages. Men have trusted God instead of scientifically mastering nature's law-abiding forces and achieving their ends by their own knowledge and skill. Men have made of God a place of soft retreat, imagining themselves in "the everlasting arms" when they should have been grappling with life's realities. Men have laid on God the responsibility of having made the world in the first place and of carrying it on to a successful issue, whereas, so humanists think, nobody made the world and nobody will make a success of it if we do not. From all reliance on superhuman aid the humanist turns away. He essays a definite and final break, not from an old to a new theology, but from any theology to none at all. He draws a circle around man's spiritual life, personal and social, on this planet and proposes that religion shall stay at home within that compass and mind its business.

No one, however deep his instinctive prejudice against such humanism, or his reasoned objection to it, should underrate its appeal. Its appearance now is no accident. It focuses a large amount of modern thought. It seems to its adherents—as ideas congenial with the Zeitgeist always seem—the inevitable corollary of intelligence. From Roman Catholicism to Protestantism to liberalism to humanism appears to them the predestined path of religious progress.

The humanist counts his advantages with gusto and gratitude and becomes missionary in his desire to share them with his fellows. The conflict between science and religion is over for him. He can even outdo the scientists in accepting a thoroughgoing mechanistic world-view. Ascribing the theism of physicists like Eddington, Millikan, and Michael

Pupin to departmentalized and uncoördinated minds, he can take it for granted that the universe is a vast, physical machine of one kind or another and that, anyway, religion is not concerned with the nature of it.

The psychological attack on religion passes him by. According to that, religion is an array of comforting wish-fulfilments by which we cushion this intolerably ruthless universe. If folk cannot endure life as it really is they can imaginatively shape it nearer to their hearts' desire by supposing that God is good, that he cares for them, and that heaven lies ahead. This alluring dream-world the humanist throws away. He has girded himself courageously to face reality and he thinks he knows it for what it is—ruthless, careless of personality, making and unmaking us with equal apathy, and at its best neutral in the struggle for spiritual values. At that point, instead of being crushed, he feels liberated—challenged, if there be no other life, to "pitch this one high!"

The humanist, therefore, is often tonic and stimulating. He can write high-minded books in which those who, like himself, have been disillusioned about the nature of the universe, are nevertheless encouraged to find spiritual values here and causes worth disinterested service.

In particular, humanism has the allurement currently associated with anything which is not too optimistic. Whatever to-day is cheering and hopeful is in so far suspect. In novel, drama, or essay on philosophy, only when one is unpleasantly realistic and grim, when one faces the seamy side, considers ugly facts, and in general appears afraid of no unpalatable conclusion does one have the accent of truth. Put side by side a typical sentence of Browning, "God! Thou art love! I build my faith on that," and a sentence from Bertrand Russell, "Omnipotent matter rolls on its relentless way," and even if no time had been given to serious thought about the relative merits of the conflicting philosophies, the second would sound to many modern ears more solid. At least, Bertrand Russell cannot be accused of fooling himself with desirable optimisms, and Browning can.

This advantage of saying forthrightly that the universe cares no more for us than the climate does for the pine trees humanism possesses. It is manifestly the credo of folks who are not spoofing.

II

Nevertheless, many who are as anxious to avoid spoofing as the sternest humanist are persuaded that humanism in the end will prove a tentative makeshift. No matter how glamorously the immediate spiritual values in man's experience are played up, and how rousingly we, biological accidents in a purposeless universe, are challenged to pitch this life high, the plain fact is that the universe is not negligible, that humanists have their theory, however disguised, about its nature and meaning, and that the logical implications of that theory are bound to become explicit.

The world-view on which the sort of humanism now under discussion is based is not, in the old sense, materialistic. The humanists are far too intelligent not to know that whatever matter may turn out to be it is much less simple than the pebbly atoms of which the cosmos once was supposed to be constructed. But they do start with a universe basically non-psychical, non-personal, non-spiritual. In its creative elements, however physics may ultimately describe them, the universe in their eyes is not intelligent, purposive, or friendly. All such attributes, excepting their presence in the animals, are exclusively human; they exist only within ourselves who happen to be alive upon the earth, and they reveal nothing about the nature of the cosmos outside of us. If we suppose they do, the humanist says, we are only clothing the naked physics of the world with our fantasies.

If one argue that the universe does apparently care for personality in the sense at least that it has produced personality, maintains it, and provides the sustenance and circumstance for its progressive achievement, the answer of the humanist is ready. The universe is to us as the sea is to the fish that live in it. The sea has indeed furnished conditions favorable to their emergence but it does not care for them. Purposively speaking, they are an accident. So far as the sea's interest is concerned, their death and birth are equally fortuitous, and the ocean is as apathetic to the extinction of a whole species as to its emergence.

In a cosmos thus negligent of human values personality has evolved and will ultimately perish— such is the basic philosophy on which non-theistic humanism proposes to erect a "high religion."

III

That misgivings are in order about such a creedal basis for religion seems clear. For humanism does not avoid a creed—its basic theory of the universe is non-theistic—and at this point of doctrine, humanism, like many another religion, faces peril. If it could remain a movement of protest merely, attacking the ignorance of orthodoxy, the compromises of liberalism, the supernatural sanctions of morality, and the weak and silly uses to which great ideas like "God" have familiarly been put, it might continue to sweep the intelligent into its stream. But the logic of events is too much for it; it is compelled increasingly to reveal its own philosophy, to become in its turn not an assailer of others' doctrines but a defender of its own; and the creed which humanists so easily assume is not by any means so easily defensible.

To begin at the most obvious point, the attitude of nonchalance toward the universe, as though so long as we have our spiritual values here the nature of the cosmos does not matter, is a pose which cannot permanently be maintained, much less be made the basis of a high religion. To be sure, the endeavor of the humanists to sustain an eager idealism despite the senseless and purposeless nature of their universe is admirable. One's faith in humankind is strengthened whenever men, facing an undesirable estate, tighten their belts to make the best of it; and this the humanists do. Unable to accept theism, in any of its forms, failing to discover in the cosmic process intelligence, purpose, or good will, they propose to take what they find standing up, not lying down. Man may be only "the disease of the agglutinated dust," but, the humanist would say, Accept the odds, be indifferent to the uneven chances of the human microcosm in the ruthless macrocosm and play the game while it lasts. All of which is high-spirited and chivalrous, but the logic of the situation will prove too much, even for such a gallant pose.

The universe is not negligible. It is insistently present, obviously immense; whatever reality is at the heart of it is the determiner of destiny. Gestures of nonchalance in the face of it are not appropriate. Repeated often enough, they begin to lose their glamour of gallantry and to become funny.

The humanist is frequently amused at the Christian. Living in a cosmos so vast that light from extra-galactic nebulæ has been traveling 186,000 miles a second for over 140,000,000 years to reach us, the Christian, nevertheless, believes with Haldane, of Oxford, that "personality is the great central fact of the universe." This seems to the humanist amusing. The emergence of personality, he thinks, is a fortuitous inadvertence on a midget planet lost in the immensities of stellar space, and Christian faith in the primacy of personality involves an utter and even humorous lack of perspective.

The Christian, on the other hand, may well discover the humor of the situation in the humanist rather than in himself. For a tiny microcosm to face this vast macrocosm with a gesture of nonchalance is, after all, sheer posing. It is striking an attitude which becomes the more incongruous the longer one watches it. If ever a religious movement whistled to keep its courage up—and many of them have—humanism does it when it proposes as a basic credo that the universe is not intelligent, purposive, or friendly, that it made us by accident and will annihilate us by necessity, but that, after all, this does not matter, that we should be disinterested about it and indifferent to it, and should proceed with eager devotion to construct a high religion.

Already the nemesis of such an attitude comes on apace. Even while Mr. Lippmann was writing *A Preface to Morals* Mr. Joseph Krutch was writing *The Modern Temper.* It is one of the most thoroughgoing statements of the implications of atheism that we have—the work of a man discontented with gestures of indifference toward the cosmos and determined to carry his philosophy through to its logical conclusions.

What Mr. Krutch sees, the humanist movement needs seriously to take to heart. Whenever anybody assumes mechanistic naturalism as a complete account of reality, he has a universe basically physical and, therefore, quantitative. He may call the creative elements electrons, mass-points, energy-units, or what not, but they are quantitative: they can be measured in terms of force and motion. The real world, however, in which we experientially live, is also qualitative. The loveliness of landscapes, the freshness of morning in the mountains, color, taste, harmony, the affections of friendship, the lure of ideals, the thrill of discovered truth, faith in the spiritual significance of life—such qualitative experiences give human existence its worth. But if the universe is basically physical and quantitative all such experiences are merely subjective; they exist only in and for ourselves; all of them are clothing which we have cut and fitted according to our own desires to dress this naked world; the cosmos itself has no quality, knows nothing of it in any form, cares nothing for it; says Mr. Krutch, "Living is merely a physiological process with only a physiological meaning."

In the world, therefore, which non-theistic humanism presupposes, not simply religion but all idealism, of whatever kind, Mr. Krutch sees the end of. Man, he writes, has "no reason to suppose that his own life has any more meaning than the life of the humblest insect that crawls from one annihilation to another." In such a world the more men and nations rise in the moral scale, the worse off they are because the more alien they become to the utterly quantitative cosmos in which they live, so that all spiritual excellence is ultimately suicidal. In such a world the romantic glamour that we have thrown around love and friendship is as much a compensatory mirage as is our faith in God; and our conceptions of chivalric honor and sacrificial devotion are as illogical as our hopes of heaven. In such a world even science can suggest nothing better to Mr. Krutch than a chapter on "The Disillusion with the Laboratory." In a word, the assumption that the cosmos is basically quantitative means to him that all the qualitative aspects of our lives are subjective fantasy, and the upshot of that situation he finds in a "moral nihilism which is fatal to society or that spiritual despair which falls upon the individual victim of an all-embracing materialistic philosophy."

I do not mean that in all this Mr. Krutch is logically infallible. I suspect that he overdraws his case. The universe may as a whole be purposeless and yet there may be purposes on earth worth living for. Certainly multiplying disciples of Mr. Krutch would not be healthy for society. Far better to have men flock to the humanists. They are right in maintaining that ethics can exist without religion and that even if there were no God we still ought to live the good life and seek fulfilment of all the possibilities in sight for ourselves and others. Nevertheless, in their too chipper assumption that we can be disinterested in the presence of a ruthless, materialistic cosmos, the humanists commonly trifle with serious matters which Mr. Krutch at least faces with candor and thoroughness. Atheism does more than negate religious faith; it makes wide areas of man's qualitative life a pathetic wish-fulfilment of alien organisms stranded in a merely quantitative world. One turns from these too easy-going and sentimental humanists to salute one of our foremost scientists who, holding the basic position on which humanism rests, said to a friend of mine, "The most tragic event in the history of the universe is that man should ever have become conscious of himself."

After all, the genesis of humanism is not difficult to see. In a generation when the older forms of theism have gone to pieces, men of high spirit and devoted enthusiasms cannot because of that stop living well. Therefore, they have dared an attitude as the only immediate recourse at hand in their emergency. They have said, Let theism go; God or no God, the good life may still be ours. As a temporary stance in a theologically slippery generation, one may not only understand that but respect it. Were I to lose my faith in God I would accept it. But it is no permanent stopping place. The difficulty of the position is already clear, even to the vanguard of those who hold its theory. If we are ultimately to save the qualitative life of man, the way through is not a tentative humanism but a reconstructed and improved theism.

IV

The difficulty of maintaining the humanistic pose with any self-content becomes even more clear when one considers the intellectual culs-de-sac into which its basic credo leads. The mental process by which the humanistic philosophy is reached is clear. First, one splits the cosmos in two with "us" on one side and the "not us" on the other. Second, one assumes that by the subtle organization of its substance, the "not us" produced "us," so that we are the result of structuralized physical elements. Third, one assumes that the physical and biological sciences, by their analysis of the "not us," are getting back to the creative factors, molecules, atoms, electrons, protons, or what not, whose various combinations make everything from stellar systems to the cortex of the human brain. Fourth, one assumes that the "not us" has done all this blindly, without anything that can be called intelligence or purpose, blundering up from star dust to man. Finally, one discovers oneself in a world where our human spirits with their conscious experience of intelligence, love, hope, faith, and aspiration, are surrounded by a vast, unconscious universe of which our spiritual values reveal nothing and to which they mean nothing. In such a situation, where, as one man put it, "we must make the best of a bad mess," humanism rises to assure us that all is not lost and that it is still possible to be nonchalant about the cosmos and high-minded in the midst of it.

To say that such a mental process fairly bristles with difficulties is to put the case mildly.

For example, behind the glowing calls of the humanists to spiritual quality and social service there is one prevailing picture of the universe: in the beginning force—non-moral, non-purposive, unintelligent force—from the blind combinations of whose energy-units the physical cosmos, its biological organisms, and its human personalities have emerged. Theoretically there are other substitutes for theism, but practically the overwhelming proportion of non-theistic minds to-day become not pantheists, panpsychists, or monists, but mechanistic naturalists. Often they do not call themselves that. Often they do not know what they are. But when one penetrates the fog of current humanism's philosophical uncertainties one generally finds, explicit or assumed, the world-view of the mechanistic naturalists. They reduce the world of spiritual values to the functioning of human personality; they reduce personality to its organism; they reduce the organism to its component physical elements; they posit behind these physical elements a world of energy-units working in mechanistic patterns— and then, slyly ascribing to these energy-units the attributes necessary to produce everything from solar systems to Christ, they accept the result as a causal explanation of the cosmos. As a matter of fact, by that process they have explained nothing; they merely have analyzed something.

The real problem of the cosmos is the whole cosmos, including man, his spiritual experience, scientific achievements, and social progress, his enriching ideals and faiths; and to abstract from this cosmic total, first, all spiritual life, then all biological organism, then all visible elements, until, left with hypothetical energy-units, we endow them with the causal capacity fortuitously to get together into the cosmic total we started with, may for certain purposes be useful analysis but it assuredly is a naïve philosophy.

When applied, for example, to an individual like William Shakspere, this method of explanation by abstraction reveals its over-simple nature. For, first, we must abstract from the total fact of Shakspere the rich intellectual and spiritual world in which he thought he lived, and must call that the functioning and, in part, the fantasy of his personality. Then we must abstract further the conscious, creative mental life of Shakspere, reducing it all, after the manner of the extreme behaviorists, to the activity of his physical organism. Then we must abstract his organism also, reducing that to its component cells, some seventy kilograms of material, getting rid of which in turn by another abstraction, we shall have left hypothetical energy-units whose fortunate though fortuitous combination was responsible for "Hamlet."

Obviously, this is not a process of explanation at all, but a process of abstraction; it is a clever way of pretending to deal with a problem by getting rid of it. Yet this same mental procedure is involved in the popular world-view which to-day obsesses the imagination of many, even among the intelligentsia.

One does not mean that the humanists are to be blamed for not having solved the problem of causation. Nobody has solved it. The theist least of all would claim to have answered adequately such ultimate philosophical questions. But the humanist is to be blamed for assuming a solution, taking it for granted as a matter of course, constructing a religion on the basis of it, and calling the result, as one of the humanists does, "the only possible kind of religion for all modern men." If such dogmatism may be matched on the other side, I should venture to be sure that no theory which represents the universe as merely *pushed up* from below by its own component energy-units without *pull* akin to intelligent purpose to supply pattern or structure can ever permanently hold the philosophic field.

Humanism is easily understandable on practical grounds. It is precisely what the humanists charge Christianity with being—an escape-mechanism. It is a refuge from a difficult situation, a demand born out of passionate human need that life shall be worthful no matter what the cosmic truth may be. As such, one sympathizes with it. One even rejoices that men and women who are unable to believe in God can yet believe in the good life and courageously undertake to live it. In Dean Sperry's figure, they are like folk who, finding that the great theistic systems have suffered shipwreck, have taken to the lifeboats; and while one recognizes that lifeboats are a temporary recourse and not a permanent establishment, one is glad to see that for the time being they are still afloat.

Indeed, humanism in its practical import deserves much more positive appreciation. Religion in America does desperately need to be humanized. The most appalling thing about some of our churches is that they are not interested in spiritual life. They are concerned with theological opinions, liturgical observances, sectarian partitions; but spiritual life is largely outside their régime. For spiritual life in our communities includes fine music, play-spaces for the children, good drama, adequate schools, beautiful homes. It counts nothing that is human alien to it. Whatever elevates life, beautifies it with significance, makes its appreciation of nature keener, its happiness in art richer, its moral practices more wholesome, its social relationships more humane is spiritual. Whatever gives men creative joy in their work, redeems life from drudgery and baptizes it with purposeful meaning is spiritual. Wherever men find in life not simply things that serve them but values which they serve, so that they are ennobled by devotion, purified by a real and inward worship of the Divine made concrete in an experience of goodness, truth, or beauty, they are winning spiritual life. Alike individuals enslaved under carnal and sordid tastes and our secular civilization as a whole, now being woven by the all-powerful machine, above all else need thus to be lifted into spiritual life. This, says the humanist, is the function of religion.

If this were humanism's primary meaning, what intelligent man would not support it? If this were humanism's exclusive meaning, who would not proudly bear its name?

When, therefore, one of the wiser humanists says of his movement that it "is not necessarily anti-theistic," we eagerly agree. We assert further that it would better not be anti-theistic. The anti-theism of current humanism is its least defensible point. For humanists traveling that road come face to face with all the difficulties which materialism, however sublimated, has always faced, and in the end they will find themselves not primarily engaged in spiritualizing life but in defending an extraordinarily credulous creed.

Of course, what all humanists desire to escape is supernaturalism, but in this they have the cordial agreement of a great body of theists. Supernaturalism is an obsolete word and it stands for an obsolete idea. Its history displays its irrelevancy to modern thought. Starting with a whimsical world, where everything that occurred was the direct volition of a human or an extrahuman agent, mankind has laboriously discovered a natural world, observed its regularities, plotted its laws, and as one area after another has thus been naturalized, the supernatural inevitably has shrunk. It has become the limbo of the as yet inexplicable, a concept with which we cover our ignorance. The partition of our world into a natural order overlaid by a supernatural order which keeps breaking through is to a well-instructed mind impossible.

When, however, the humanist and the theist together have thus got rid of the false distinction—natural versus supernatural—they still have on their hands the real distinction—physical versus spiritual. Both physical things and spiritual values are actually here. They are indisputable facts. Something must be done with them. Can it be that physical things alonè are basically real and creative, and that spiritual values are epiphenomenal—casual, inexplicable, subjective accidents, revelatory of nothing beyond themselves? That is the creed to which antitheistic humanism is consenting. It would better not consent. There are rough seas ahead of that philosophy.

V

The most serious difficulty with humanism is that it undercuts the very thing it tries to do. It seriously desires to save the good life in a godless world and it wishes to pitch that life in a high key. When the humanist talks ethics, the modern Christian finds himself listening to a familiar tune in which he easily can join. Like the religious liberal, the humanist maintains old virtues, which in every generation have enriched personality, and pleads for fresh ventures of the moral sense in situations where "new occasions teach new duties."

Indeed, deprived of God, with nothing left from the race's heritage of idealistic philosophy and religious faith except the good life, humanists do sometimes so specialize in that and give creative thought to it that they render distinguished service in the very field where on *a priori* grounds the theist expects to see them fail. For this reason one of our professorial agnostics wishes that we could declare a moratorium on God for forty years and see if without theology we might not be morally improved. One who is himself a theist would better take to heart such current distrust of theism's ethical consequence. The influence of much of our popular belief in God is not moral but immoral. It means a lazy shouldering off on a kindly deity of tasks we must perform ourselves. It means stereotyped concepts of right and wrong, defined by infallible revelation and unadjustable to new demands. It, therefore, anesthetizes its devotees and checks instead of encourages creative thought on personal and social morals. The humanists are right in much of their attack on current theism and the theist would better be the first to acknowledge it.

Nevertheless, the matter is not so simple that it

can be disposed of by the humanist's moratorium on God. Ultimately an ethic of high ideals supported with enthusiastic and unflagging devotion does not depend on the supernatural dictation of a code or on a system of divine rewards and punishments, or on a picture of God as king, lawgiver, and judge, or on infallible authority in church or Bible, or on anything else against which the humanist launches his favorite attacks, but it does depend on reverence for personality. There is the crux of the whole matter. Right and wrong are basically a scale of values; ideas concerning them depend on what the individual and the society he lives in regard as valuable; and ultimately morals, considering how persons should live in an intermeshing network of personal relationships, depend on personality's worth.

Nor is it possible to boom the worth of personality by willing it, to insist that it shall be worthful though the heavens fall. No fiat-value can be created in personality by any humanist's edict. Here he must take the consequences of his cosmic creed; here in spite of himself the background of his thought crowds up into the foreground. Personality a fortuitous by-product of a careless universe, its mental and spiritual life revealing nothing beyond itself, its finest faiths comforting fantasies by which it escapes from the world of fact to the world of desire, its source self-motivating energy-units, its history an interlude between two annihilations, its ultimate future without hope—so in his basic philosophy the non-theistic humanist rates personality. To suppose that such an estimate has no ethical repercussions is incredible. They may be postponed in the individual humanist but they will ultimately emerge out of his movement as a whole.

Indeed they already are emerging. The same generation which sees humanism positing a godless world and trying to preserve the good life in it sees increasing numbers of people in the same godless world drawing logical conclusions as to its meaning. Our modern novelists say forthrightly what they think. One of them almost is persuaded that he is "only a bundle of cellular matter upon its way to become manure." Writes another, "We don't matter. Man matters only to himself. He is fighting a lone fight against a vast indifference." Our modern essayists are not reticent about the corollaries of a godless world. Writes Mr. Krutch, "Ours is a lost cause and there is no place for us in the natural universe." Even Mr. Lippmann, when in a burst of confidence he canvasses the possibilities of personal meaning in the cosmos as he sees it, says that life may be a "comedy, or high tragedy, or plain farce."

It should be noted that all such judgments do not

primarily concern God; they concern human personality. They move in the realm of ethics. They interpenetrate a man's estimate of himself and of the whole world of persons. They drag the creed of humanism out of the realm of cosmic theory into the realm of the good life, which humanists wish to maintain. Here lies the difficulty of a successful humanism: it sucks the egg of personality's value and then tries to hatch a high religion out of it.

One device by which this consequence is warded off is the attempt to hold a milder and more tolerable opinion of the physical universe's relationship to man. Instead of emphasizing Bertrand Russell's thoroughgoing view of the situation, "Brief and powerless is Man's life; on him and all his race the slow, sure doom falls pitiless and dark," some humanists prefer to call the cosmos neutral. It assumes in their imagination an almost benign aspect as though, providing the setting for the human game, furnishing the material with which the game may be played, and laying down the rules, it stood aside to let individuals in particular and the race in general win if they can. In such a view as this, however, the human fantasy is obviously at work elaborating its wish-fulfilments. For whatever words may legitimately be used to describe the relationship of the cosmos with man, neutrality is not among them. If human personality is a trivial incident in the history of the colossal macrocosm, the macrocosm will not in the end be neutral in dealing with man's cherished interests and values. Against the background of stellar time, the rise and dissolution of solar systems is like the freezing and melting of seasonal ice on earthly rivers; and so far from being able to trust the cosmos for benignant neutrality, the thoroughgoing non-theistic mind must foresee the ultimate disintegration of everything that man has hoped or planned. "Nothing will remain," says one frank scientist, "not even the ruins." In such a world our personal values are our subjective writing on the cosmic slate, and in the end the universe will wipe them off and then smash the slate.

The humanist's non-theistic picture of the cosmos, therefore, necessarily involves a value-judgment about man. Say as one will that what man is he is, whatever may be his cosmic origin, and that the worth of personality is an empirical fact to be discovered by experiment, it still is true that if one starts with the judgment that basically "personality is the great central fact of the universe," one moves out to a corresponding level of expectation, but that if one starts with the judgment that basically "living is merely a physiological process with only a physiological meaning," one naturally moves out to another level altogether.

This, as I understand it, is what belief in God is all about. We are not anxious concerning God because, for its own sake, we hunger and thirst after a cosmic theory. Multitudes do not so hunger in the least, and few of us do much of the time. What does matter to us, however, day in and day out, is the value of personality. How much we ourselves are ultimately worth, what possibilities we may reasonably believe resident in human personality at large, whether the progress already observable from the Neanderthal man up is a trifling cosmic inadvertence or is prophetic of resident potentialities in man's spiritual life with divine resources behind them—this is an intimate, penetrating matter which affects daily living. To say that personality is the child of the Eternal Spirit, in very truth the great central fact of the universe, is one thing; to say that personality is a chance spark struck off from physical collisions is another. Let no humanist content himself with pretense in this matter: that difference involves prodigious ethical results.

Nor may this difficulty be avoided by the substitution of agnosticism for atheism. Maybe God is, some humanists would say, maybe not; concerning that be disinterested; in the meantime we have the

good life. Such agnosticism, however, does not escape
the question of personality's value. No one can be
altogether agnostic about that. "What a man believes," writes George Bernard Shaw, "may be
ascertained not from his creed, but from the assumptions on which he habitually acts." Now, no assumptions on which we habitually act are more
unavoidable than the estimates of human value that
interpenetrate our conduct. From our treatment of
our children to our belief about the possibility of
ending war, attitudes toward personality, estimates
of it, and convictions concerning it consciously or
unconsciously enter into our behavior. On one side
are those who think that when human history is
finished it will prove to have been "a brief and
transitory episode in the life of one of the meanest
of the planets." On the other side are those who
think that man is a child of God, with the possibilities and destinies which that involves. In between
are the humanists, trying to keep foothold on both
positions, endeavoring to combine a high estimate of
life's spiritual worth and eventual significance with
the positive belief or the strong suspicion that personality is a casual phenomenon like phosphorescence
in the sea. It is not an easy position to maintain.
God is not so readily got rid of without being
missed.

One thing the humanist tries to forget but must in the end remember: theism is a value-judgment as to the worth and meaning of personality.

To be sure, current popular theism cannot be maintained. The old theistic systems are indeed going to pieces. Many of the hymns, sermons, admonitions, rituals, and liturgies which sprang out of them are already in the eyes and ears of the intelligent obsolete, save as, like the stories of the Greek pantheon, they are given poetic interpretation. The final answer which the theist must make to the humanist is not complaint against the tentative unsatisfactoriness of his position, but the positive presentation of a credible idea of God. In the meantime, amid the mass of undigested factual material which modern religion faces, the thoughtful theist knows that he often appears vague in his idea of deity. He frankly despairs of tossing off on demand a statement of theism philosophically adequate to this new, amazing universe. He sees in that task work for many minds demanding more than one generation, but he is still convinced that atheism is no solution of the problem and that behind our partial and inadequate ideas of God is God.

Were I personally to lose that confidence, undoubtedly I should try to be a humanist. I should agree that even when all spiritual meaning is banished from ultimate reality, and the things that we love best—friendship, poetry, science, societies that grow in humaneness and good will—are seen as trivial incidents in the colossal onrush of the cosmos, it still is better to love those values and find one's life in their service. I should honestly endeavor to be a courageous humanist, counting it craven to let even an antagonistic universe dissuade me from decency, justice, and good will. But in hours of lucid insight when I grasped the full-orbed meaning of the idea that the determiner of destiny is altogether physical, no more aware of our human values than are the stars of the Big Dipper that they look to us like a human instrument, I should be a far-from-enthusiastic humanist. Not that I expect any God there is to nurse me here or furnish me a diadem hereafter! On any sane philosophy this universe is engaged in a business too vast to be solicitous about merely individual desires. But in a world basically quantitative, not individual desires alone, supra-individual personal values—goodness, truth, beauty—are denied any cosmic rootage and are left to find what nourishment they can without it, assured that in the end they all will perish in the planet's decease. In such a world I know that the level of my ideals for human life inevitably would sink. I should attempt less and expect less. Recognizing all our qualitative experience as transient foliage with which we clothe the bare rock of a quantitative world, it would be impossible to keep the grim, craggy fact from showing through. I should know beyond a peradventure that the spiritual heroes whose faith and sacrifice have lifted and illumined our humanity never could have built their lives on that hypothesis. There would be hours when I, a humanist, would pray to the God I no longer believed in to help theists so credibly to rebuild theism that humanists might disappear.

Are Religious People Fooling Themselves?

A FRESH criticism of religion is afoot, the subtlety of which makes it difficult to counter. The gist of the contention is that religion is a comforting fantasy. Finding ourselves in a ruthless universe, so we are told, we imagine an illusory world of divine mercy and care and, thus making our existence more tolerable, we cling to the subterfuge as a sacred possession.

A wife who discovered that she had been worshiping an imaginative construct of her husband instead of seeing clearly the real nature of the man, once broke down in my presence with the cry, "For all these years I have supposed myself sincerely loved, but I was only fooling myself." Many to-day entertain a similar suspicion about their relations with the universe. They have believed it to be the work of a merciful God; they have seen it unified by divine purpose and illumined by divine love; they have prayed to their God, sung songs about him, found comfort and stimulation through faith in him. Now, however, they wonder whether they are not fooling themselves. Is not religion the supreme example of the way mankind can enjoy an illusion?

It is time to expect this particular difficulty to arise. The physical and biological sciences have been causing such radical readjustments of religious thought as will leave Christianity hardly recognizable by an ancient devotee but, while badly needing hospitalization in consequence, religion has kept its banners flying. The new universe of staggering distances is far less cozy a setting for the religious imagination to operate in than the old cosmology afforded, but it will take more than the new astronomy to banish God. Evolution has done to death some precious myths but, while landing painfully on sensitive spots, its weapons have not reached the heel of Achilles. The mathematical mechanism of natural processes has put religious thought on its mettle, but, as was pointed out long ago, hats made by machinery still fit human heads and a railroad train, mechanistic if anything is, still goes somewhere; mechanism and purpose are not antithetical, and a world of mechanistic processes may still be grounded in intelligence and guided by an aim.

The fresh criticism of religion starts where these old difficulties leave off. It asks why men so pertinaciously desire religious faith and so pugnaciously refuse to give it up. It inquires why religion exhibits such infinite capacity to recuperate from apparently fatal illnesses and even to revive after its obsequies have been publicly announced. This continuous ability of religion to escape from tight places, assume new forms, and settle down in strange intellectual environments must have an explanation within the nature of man himself. Man thus clings to religion, the solution runs, because he needs it. He needs it because the real universe is a Gargantuan physical process, which cares nothing for man or his values, knows nothing of him, and in the end will snuff him out. This world of fact is so intolerable that man refuses to live in it until he has overlayed it with a world of desire. Religion is thus a comforting illusion. It survives, not because it is true, but precisely because it is false; it is the world as man would like it, imaginatively superimposed on the world as it really is.

To be sure, this reduction of theology to psychology is not new; more than once in the long, running fight between religion and irreligion the completely subjective nature of God has been asserted, as, for example, by Feuerbach in the last century, but to-day this old method of attack has gained fresh poignancy. When it is Freudian, it posits the experience of the babe in his mother's womb as the most comfortable epoch in the human organism's existence—an experience of such sheltering care that unconsciously the adult forever wishes to return. Religion, then, with its God of love, is a psychological wish-fulfilment; it springs from the pathetic longing of the human organism in this inexorable universe to retreat to solace and peace.

No such special formulation, however, is indispensable to the interpretation of religious faith as a consoling mirage. Whether the mechanism by which it emerges is phrased in Freudian terms or not, faith can still be charged with being an illusion. Never did religion face hostile strategy more threatening. In the most dangerous hours of ascendent disbelief, when man's faith has been assailed as irrational and obsolete, it still has been possible to marshal evidence of the serviceable effects of religion on its believers, to enlarge on the comfort it confers, the doors of hope it opens, the sense of life's significance it imparts, the stimulating faiths it furnishes, the lives it invigorates and transforms. Now, however, all this is turned against the defenders of the faith.

To be sure, says the rejoinder, religion is comforting, stimulating, encouraging. That is the reason why folk are religious. This universe, seen as modern science reveals it, is utterly without encouragement or comfort.

> The world rolls round for ever like a mill;
> It grinds out death and life and good and ill;
> It has no purpose, heart or mind or will.

In such a cosmos the naked facts are too unendurably inhuman to be sustained with equanimity or lived upon with eagerness. But human beings, fortuitously emerging on this transient planet and living, as one astronomer puts it, like sailors who run up the rigging of a sinking ship, passionately desire to be at peace and to work with enthusiasm. Therefore, they make up religion. It springs from unconscious processes of emotional reaction. It is comparable to our concealment of the uncomfortable process of gestation under the friendly figure of the stork. It is the human organism's way of looking in another direction when the truth becomes intolerable, and there seeing what he wants to see. Religion no longer needs to be disproved; it is merely a psychological process to be explained.

By this strategy of attack some of the most potent religious artillery falls into the hands of the enemy. The more we insist on the beauty and usefulness of religious faith and extol it as a way to abundant living, the worse off, apparently, we are, for the more we lend color to the contention that religion rests on subjective desire rather than on objective fact. Thus losing so large a portion of our offensive armament, we find ourselves, as well, blasted from old defensive citadels. For in the past, no matter how difficult the intellectual readjustments may have been, we could insist that though God cannot be proved he cannot be disproved, that the path of faith is open to belief in a spiritual interpretation of the world. Now, however, the vanguard of the irreligious have no interest in disproving God; they simply explain him—he is a defense-mechanism by which we make a pitiless universe seem fatherly, a subjective fog-bank, hiding cruel facts of the real world, by calling which solid ground we make life more livable.

II

The first reaction of a religious man to this subtle and serious attack would better be frank recognition of the truth in it. Anyone acquainted with even the environs of modern psychiatry knows that not only religious imagination but every other function of the human mind is commonly used as a means of substituting desire for reality. "Anything to escape, to colour the spectacles!" exclaims one of Warwick Deeping's characters. The psychiatrist suspects that human life is largely lived on that basis. Defense-mechanisms, rationalizations, and wish-fantasies, by which we sidestep the actual and escape into some desired fairyland, abound in the human mind. Indeed, tricks of evasion and self-deceit so infest our thinking that their presence in religion is only a small portion of the total problem which they represent.

"As one runs through the literature of the psychiatrist and the psychoanalyst of the day," writes Professor Gault, "one gains the impression that much of our behavior and almost every emotional reaction that one experiences is a defense." Drunkenness is a defense-mechanism by which we escape from humdrum conditions; boasting a compensatory device by which we elude a real sense of inferiority and simulate a superior attitude; day-dreams a means of flight from a world of tiresome fact to a world of desire; hysteria a form of subconscious shirking; and a Micawberish faith that something will turn up, a familiar psychological alibi for directive thinking and hard work. The most difficult task in the world for most people is courageously to deal with reality. Our sanitariums are full of folk who, eluding constructive handling of their factual problems, have subconsciously betaken themselves to neurasthenia until neurasthenia has taken hold on them, and any one of us intelligently watching his own mind can catch it weaving its cunning subterfuges of escape.

That is to say, the charge now made against religion, that it can be used and is being used as a substitute for facing real facts, is a charge that can be made against the whole mental life of man.

To be sure, religion is commonly employed as a means of retreat from disturbing facts! So are countless other things from cocaine, day-dreams, and detective stories, to music, poetry, and ordinary optimism. "Land sakes!" said one poor woman in Middletown, "I don't see how people live at all who don't cheer themselves up by thinkin' of God and Heaven." Many people's faith is thus a practical way of finding cheer when untoward circumstances press too ruthlessly upon them. Granted that such religion is naïve, not at all concerned with the philosophic truth about the universe, and taken for granted as a useful means of achieving solace in an uncomfortable world, one may say, even on this level, that, considering the various other defense-mechanisms popularly employed to cheer people up, we may be thankful that some folk still remain who reach the goal of inward joy by thinking about God.

While, however, this practical and largely unconsidered retreat upon religious faith because of its comforting effects is inevitably to be expected, intelligent exponents of religion cannot be complacent about the matter. Undoubtedly, many religious people are fooling themselves. Careless of the facts of the universe, they try by imaginative devices to wangle out of life a temporary peace of mind. They surround themselves with an impinging world of friendly saints and angels; believe what they wish to believe about the goodness of God, the spiritual significance of life, the hope of immortality; display militant impatience at any disturbance of their faiths and expectations. The impression they make on the detached observer is unfortunate. He is inclined to feel, like one young collegian, that "Religion is nothing but a chloroform mask into which the weak and unhappy stick their faces."

Obviously, such disparagement depends on an interpretation of religion in comfortable terms. No austere religion of self-renunciation would suggest this criticism. Our soft and sentimental modernism, therefore, must in this matter accept heavy responsibility, for it undoubtedly has led Christianity into the defile where this ambush could be sprung with deadliest effect. The old orthodoxy was by no means so susceptible of interpretation in terms of comfort. Men believed in a Calvinistic God who from all eternity had foredoomed multitudes of his children to eternal hell. Preachers drove women mad and made strong men cry out in terror by their pictures of God holding sinners over the infernal pit and likely at any moment to let go. One who, like myself, has now a long memory can recall those days when fear haunted the sanctuary. When I was seven I cried myself to sleep in dread that I was going to hell and when I was nine I was ill from panic terror lest I had committed the unpardonable sin. Had the idea been broached in those days that religion is merely a psychological device by which we solace ourselves, it would have been difficult to see the point.

Against this reign of terror in religion the new theology revolted. Judgment Day was allegorized; hell was sublimated; predestination was denied; God was sentimentalized. Whatever was harsh, grim, forbidding in the old religion was crowded to the periphery or thrust out altogether, and whatever was lovely, comforting, hopeful was made central. Religion became a song about the ideal life, the love of God, the hope of heaven. Many of the older generation still remember how like the water and bread of life this new interpretation seemed. It was part and parcel of the Zeitgeist; it accorded with the mid-Victorian attitude; it emerged in Browning's gorgeous optimism as well as in the sentimentality of gospel hymns. Skeptics might doubt and science pose difficult problems, but we knew that in this inspiring faith of religion—a good God, a morally trustworthy universe, an onward and upward march forever—we had found the secret of triumphant living. And now the ambush breaks upon this very position. Our strategy apparently has gone awry and the very battle-line we chose has given to the irreligious the best opportunity they ever had. They grant everything we say about the loveliness and comfort of our faith; they agree that it inspires, consoles, enheartens, and pacifies; they consent to the claim that it is emotionally satisfying and often practically useful. The fact that it is all this, they say, explains its emergence. It is a fantasy constructed for this very purpose. It is man's subjective method of making himself more comfortable in an uncomfortable world.

What we face to-day, therefore, is not only the universal tendency in human nature to sugarcoat stern fact with fantasy, but this tendency accentuated by a type of religion which lends itself readily to such saccharine use. The upshot is that multitudes of religious people are unquestionably fooling themselves. The chief engineer of the Eighth Avenue Subway recently told me that he had received a letter from a woman demanding that the blasting on the subway be stopped because it interfered with the singing of her pet canary. That woman's outlook illustrates much popular religion. Her ego had pushed itself into the center of the city's life; her pet canary's singing had become to her a crucial matter of metropolitan concern; the vast enterprises of the municipality should in her opinion turn aside for her pet. A similar frame of mind characterizes egocentric religion.

To be sure, some two billion years ago this little planet broke off from its parent sun and started on its orbit of six hundred million miles. To be sure, the sun itself is but a tiny thing—millions of it could be lost in a star like Betelgeuse. The cosmos is a blasting operation on a titanic scale. This fact does not shut out the possibility that the Power behind the universe may ultimately be interested in personality. The Eighth Avenue Subway is concerned with personality; the welfare of persons is its object. Individual whimsies, however, do not count; pet canaries are not determinative. So our universe is a stern affair, and the God of it, as Jesus said in his parable, is like an "austere man." He has no pets, he plays no favorites, he stops no blasting for any man's canary. Law rules in this cosmos, not magic. There are no Aladdin's lamps. To forget that is to run with the egocentric multitude into a religion of illusion.

It is one thing, however, thus to grant that religious imagination, like every other mental functioning, is used to produce egotistically satisfying fantasies; it is another thing to claim that so obvious a fact finally disposes of religion. The latter is a much more weighty proposition than can be supported by any psychoanalysis of religious wish-fulfilments.

III

The claim that religion essentially is fantasy is just as strong or weak as the materialistic worldview with which it starts. For whether explicit or not, materialism, by whatever special name it may now be called to distinguish it from discredited predecessors, supplies these new strategists with their base of operations. They begin with a merely quantitative universe; they assume its metrical aspects to be original and creative; the cosmos, in their view, has emerged from the automatic organization of physical energy-units. With this for their beginning, their ending is inevitable; all man's qualitative life —his disinterested love of truth, beauty, and goodness—is purely subjective. In so far as his mind discovers quantitative facts, man may be knowing the outer world somewhat as it really is, but when, so we are told, man tries to externalize his æsthetic and moral life, to posit a good God, or see artistry as a structural fact in the universe, or interpret social progress in terms of cosmic purpose, he is fooling himself. Nothing outside his own psychological processes corresponds with what he experiences as creative spiritual life. Since, therefore, there is no goodness, purpose, intelligence, artistry, love, or any other spiritual quality present in the universe external to man, all religion, in so far as it inspires man with the faith that his spiritual life is a revelation of the universal life, is fallacious. On that basis alone can the claim be erected that religion is essentially a fantasy. With that for a starting point one may go on to say with a character in a modern novel, "Man invents religion to hide the full horror of the universe's complete indifference, for it is horrible."

It is necessary to insist that this new psychological attack on religion does rest back on a materialistic foundation, and is just as steady or as shaky as its base. Too frequently these new stategists are unwilling to make a frank statement of their worldview. The number of thoroughgoing minds like Bertrand Russell's, believing in the final triumph of "omnipotent matter" and drawing the legitimate conclusion that religion is, of course, subjective finery with which we clothe an inexorable world, is small. Most of the humanists who elide all extrahuman elements from religion and reduce it to subjectivism discreetly draw a veil of silence over their world-view.

Once in a while some lucid mind, disliking clandestine dealing, states frankly what the upshot is to human life on this planet when his philosophy is granted. So Mr. Everett Dean Martin says: "At the end of all our strivings and efforts science sees our world a frozen clod whirling through emptiness about a cheerless and exhausted sun, bearing on its sides the marks of man's once hopeful activity, fragments of his works of art mixed with glacial débris, all waiting in the dark for millenniums until the final crash comes, when even the burned out sun shall be shattered in collision with another like it, and the story shall all be over while there is no one to remember and none to care. All will be as if it had never been." Obviously, in a universe where all spiritual values are thus casual, fortuitous, and transient, religion is an illusion. On that basis one might even say with Goncourt that "Life is a nightmare between two nothings," and add that religion is a subterfuge for inducing sweeter dreams. Most of the new strategists, however, never go through with their position to this logical conclusion but, forgetting their total world-view as best they can, play around with such optimisms as happen to intrigue them. The fact is that when it comes to indulging in defense-mechanisms and fantasies the humanists practice it quite as commonly as the theists.

One editor, for example, rather desperately trying to be a humanist, says, "We ought to push gently aside the subject of cosmology for a season, and come to ontology. Not the universe, but man, is our proper study." The picture of this editor endeavoring "gently" to get the cosmos out of sight is one of the most priceless things that recent religious discussion has produced. Unfortunately this method of retreat from reality, this legerdemain by which the cosmos is "gently" secreted from view is common. Nevertheless, the cosmos is important.

Indeed, the claim that religion is essentially a branch of pathological psychology is based upon gigantic assumptions about the cosmos. For example, it accuses the religious man who believes that the world has mind behind it and in it of constructing a fantasy to please himself, and in so doing it assumes that the world does not have mind behind it or in it, but is a potpourri and salmagundi of mindless forces. That is an immense assumption. As a matter of fact, this universe does not seem to be a nonmental process into which we import rationality as a comforting myth. The Empire State Building is no merely physical thing separable from mind; it is objectified thought. Abstract from it its mathematics, the ideas and plans which mind injected and without which it could not be understood at all, and the remainder would not be a building. The very substance of the structure, the factors that make it cohere, are mental.

The mind's relationship with the intelligible universe as a whole is not altogether different from this. All the world of things we know lies within the apprehension of our minds. The very distances between the stars exist for us in our mental measurements. The realm of science, its formulations of law and its ideas of cause and effect are not directly given in our sensations of the outer world, but exist primarily in the world of thought. It is just as true to say that the cosmos exists in our minds, as to say that our minds exist in the cosmos. So obvious is this that when Professor Jeans closes his essay, "Eos," setting forth the breath-taking marvels of modern astronomy, he describes man as an infant gazing at it all and says, "Ever the old question obtrudes itself as to whether the infant has any means of knowing that it is not dreaming all the time. The picture it sees may be merely a creation of its own mind." Personally, I doubt that, but certainly the idea that physical energy-units have merely tossed us up into existence in a chance burst of energy and that our minds are aliens here in a non-mental world, fooling themselves by thinking there is sense in it, is no adequate account of the situation. The universe as we know it is thoroughly mental.

Harry Elmer Barnes recently wrote, "Astronomically speaking, man is almost totally negligible," to which George Albert Coe whipped back an answer, " 'Astronomically speaking, man is'—the astronomer!" Quite so! There is no sense in claiming that astronomy belittles man when the astronomical universe which man marvels at is alike the discovery and the construct of man's mind.

These new strategists also accuse the religious man of wildly practicing fantasy when he reads the meaning of the cosmic process in terms of its highest revelation, personality. That accusation involves the assumption that personality is not a revelation of anything beyond itself, that while stars, rocks, and atoms are truth-tellers about the cosmos, the most significant thing we know, self-conscious being with powers of reflective thought, creative art, developing goodness, and effective purpose, has nothing to reveal. That is a gigantic assumption.

As a matter of fact, personality with its creative powers, spiritual achievements, developing civilizations, alluring possibilities, is here. However the world came into being, there must be somewhere the potency from which these consequences have emerged. "King Lear" cannot be explained by merely analyzing the play into the arithmetical points which constitute the hooks and dashes, which in turn constitute the letters, which in turn constitute the words, which in turn constitute the sentences, which in turn constitute the drama. If one tries to content oneself with such analysis, one must first by sleight of hand import into the original arithmetical points the potency of such self-motivation and self-arrangement as will bring the Shakesperean consequence. Just this the mechanistic naturalist does. When no one is looking, he slips into the universe's energy-units the potentiality—whatever that may mean—to become Plato's brain and Christ's character. If one is really desirous of getting rid of illusion one may well start with discontent at this mental legerdemain.

Such an interpretation assumes that the whole universe, including the human mind itself, is the result of casual cosmic weathering, and that any spiritual meaning supposedly found there is our fantasy. In Canon Streeter's phrase, it pictures the universe as "one gigantic accident consequent upon an infinite succession of happy flukes." As a serious attempt to understand a process which has issued in Beethoven's symphonies, Einstein's cosmology, and the Sermon on the Mount, to mention nothing else, this seems painfully inadequate.

If the universal process is thus nothing but the self-organization of physical energy, then the cortex of the human brain must be included. That also would be the result of self-organizing energy-units working in mechanistic patterns, and mental determinism is the inevitable consequence. The universal energy, arranging itself into nebulæ, solar systems, plants, and animals, has at last arranged itself into the human brain, and from the bottom to the top of this cosmic process everything is predetermined by mechanical necessity. This means that the functioning of physical cells, working in mechanistic patterns along lines of least resistance in the brain, predetermines everything we think—Freud's arguments as well as religion's answer, Voliva's idea that the earth is flat, as well as Jeans' astronomy. The mind's relation to the brain becomes, in such a case, as some have frankly said, like the shadow cast by a moving object. That is to say, all our apparent mental choices are predetermined activities of physical energy-units—not our reasoned reply to the world but only our automatic reaction.

To say that with such a world-view religion is an illusion is to state the consequence mildly; the

serious meaning of reflective thought has also disappeared into mirage.

It is the distinguished virtue of a book like Mr.
Joseph Krutch's *The Modern Temper*, that in it this
fact is so clearly recognized and so honestly stated.
Mr. Krutch is persuaded that religion is a comforting myth. It represents the world as man would like
to have it in contrast with the world as man discovers it to be. It is born of desire and is clung to
because, created by desire, it is more satisfactory than
cruel fact. Mr. Krutch, that is, joins heartily in the
new attack on religion. But he has a thoroughgoing
mind. He sees that on that basis what is true of
religion is true of all the intellectual and spiritual
faculties of man, that scientific optimism is as un-
founded as religious optimism, that not only is man
"an ethical animal in a universe which contains no
ethical element," but he is a philosophical animal
in a universe which contains no philosophical element; that all man's finer life—art, romance, sense
of honor—is as much an alien in this world as is
religion and that, if the cosmos is basically physical,
then through the entire range of man's mental and
moral experience he faces "an intolerable disharmony
between himself and the universe." This conclusion
when the premises are granted seems to me inevitable. In a merely quantitative world all qualitative

life is alien; we are then in a night where all cows are black.

If it be true that whatever arises in our experience by psychological processes in order that life may become more livable is, therefore, suspect, then everything is suspect. Of course, religion meets psychological needs! Of course that is why it has arisen and has so tenaciously persisted! Of course, if religion had not aided the survival of the human organism, it long since would have disappeared. At its best it does inspire, encourage, and enrich life; it enables men to transcend their environments, rise above them, be superior to them, and carry off a spiritual victory in the face of them. And because of this, passing through many intellectual formulations, it still abides. In this it is at one with science, love, music, art, poetry, and moral excellence. This fact alone neither credits nor discredits anything in man's experience.

The great question on the answer to which all depends still remains: *why* a universe in which beings have evolved who cannot live without such spiritual values? The extraordinary datum to be dealt with is that, as a matter of fact, personalities exist, finding life intolerable without philosophy, ethics, art, music, and religion. The cosmos has produced us, has forced us, if we are to survive on honorable terms, to develop such spiritual faculties, has set a livable life as a prize not to be won without the creation and maintenance of these higher powers. It must require a particular kind of cosmos to act that way. The fact of personality, with its intellectual and spiritual needs, is the most amazing with which the universe faces us, and no detailed analysis of psychological mechanisms can seriously affect its explanation; it is the total fact which waits to be understood. That out of the cosmos has come a being too significant to find contentment without spiritual interpretations of his life is the basic datum on which intelligent religion rests its case.

IV

The ultimate answer to the new attack, however, does not lie in the realm of intellectual discourse. The attack will continue until we popularly achieve a type of religion which does not come within its line of fire. Our real trouble is egocentric religion, which does egregiously fool its devotees. A comfortable modernism which, eliminating harsh and obsolete orthodoxies and making a few mental adjustments to scientific world-views, contents itself with a sentimentalized God and a roseate optimism will, if it continues, encourage the worst opinions of religion as a pacifying fantasy. Such a lush gospel will claim its devotees, but minds with any sinew in them turn away. Modern Christianity has grown soft, sentimental, saccharine. It has taken on pink flesh and lost strong bone. It has become too much flute and too little trumpet. It has fallen from the stimulating altitudes of austerity and rigor, where high religion customarily has walked. Its preachers have become too commonly religious crooners. In consequence it is called a mere wish-fulfilment because it acts that way. "No completely healthy intelligent person," says one of our psychologists, "who has not suffered some misfortune can ever be truly religious." That is not so much intellectual judgment as peevishness, but the writer could easily claim that he had much to be peevish about.

The only adequate answer is a kind of religion which a "completely healthy intelligent person"—if there are any such—can welcome with the consent of all his faculties. At least three elements, I think, are crucially required.

A religion in holding which a man does not fool himself must take into full account the law-abiding nature of the world. Most popular religion is not yet within sight of that goal. Just as astronomy came out of astrology and on our back streets still displays the left-overs of its ancient superstition, or as chemistry came out of alchemy and labored for centuries to throw off its old credulities, so religion came out of magic. Primitive religion was magical and primitive magic was religious. The adhesive power of magical ideas is prodigious, and millions of people in the modern world retain a magical faith. They try to use God as a short-cut to get things they want because they want them, and not at all because they have fulfilled the law-abiding conditions for getting them.

To be sure, religious men do lip-service to the reign of law. They even acclaim it and quote stock arguments by which a law-abiding world can be conceived as under the governance of God. But too seldom have they grasped in either thought or practice the basic implication of the reign of law—that nothing can be won except by fulfilling the law-abiding conditions for getting it.

Especially does this magical attitude persist in prayer. Even the plain lessons of history are lost on multitudes of pious believers. They know or ought to know the story of the plagues that once devastated the Western world and of the prayers lifted in agonized desire and faith against them. They should know also that plagues continued their recurrent terror until sanitary conditions were fulfilled, and that even to this day wherever those conditions are neglected all the frenzied petitions of magical religion are of no avail.

This is a law-abiding world in which a man may not run to God saying, "Stop your blasting for my pet canary!" It is fortunate that such is the case. A cosmos in which we received what we wanted because we wanted it without fulfilling the conditions for getting it would be a fool's world that could produce only fools. "If wishes were horses, beggars would ride."

If we desire physical results we must fulfil physical conditions; if we desire mental results we must fulfil mental conditions; if we desire spiritual results we must fulfil spiritual conditions—that simple, basic, obvious fact would revolutionize popular religion if once it were apprehended. Let the pious trust God if they will, but it is fantasy to trust him to break his own laws. All supernaturalism is illusion. Even the prescientific New Testament says, "Be not deceived; God is not mocked: for whatsoever a man soweth, that shall he also reap," which translated into modern speech means, I suppose, "Don't fool yourself; this is a law-abiding world."

Intelligent prayer in particular is not magic; it is the inward fulfilling of spiritual conditions so that appropriate spiritual results are possible. It is the very soul of personal religion, but it is not whimsical, capricious, an affair of desperate exigency expressed in spasms of appeal. It is an inward life habitually lived in such companionship that the effective consequence follows.

A man whose religion lies thus in a spiritual life which, fulfilling spiritual conditions in a law-abiding spiritual world, achieves triumphant spiritual results, is not fooling himself.

Another element is bound to characterize a religious experience which escapes illusion—self-renunciation. The egocentric nature of much popular religion is appalling. The perspective is all wrong. Even God becomes a matter of interest to many believers largely for what they can get out of him. They treat the Deity as a kind of universal valet to do odds and ends for them, a sort of "cosmic bellboy" for whom they push buttons, and who is expected to come running. "God for us," is the slogan of their faith, instead of, "Our lives for God."

As a result, much current religion becomes what the new attack takes it to be—an auxiliary of selfishness. The centripetal force of a selfish life, when that life becomes religious, sweeps the whole cosmos in. God himself becomes a nursemaid for our pets, and religion sinks into a comfortable faith that we shall be fondly taken care of, our wishes fulfilled, and our egocentric interests coddled. Professor Royce of Harvard used to tell his students never to look for "sugar-plums . . . in the home of the Infinite." That injunction is critically needed in contemporaneous religion. Looking for sugar-plums in the home of the Infinite is precisely what popular religion is concerned about.

All great religion, however, starts with self-renunciation and there is no great religion without it. Such faith is austere, rigorous, difficult. It promises no coddling and expects no sugar-plums. It does not use God as a *deus ex machina* which in an emergency will do our bidding; it believes in God as the source and conserver of spiritual values, and dedicates life to his service.

Strangely enough, Christianity has been and still is interpreted as the supreme example of a coddling, comfortable faith. Jesus' dominant doctrine, the sacredness of personality, given a selfish twist, leads Christians to put each his own personality into the center of the cosmos and to see the divine purposes arrange themselves in concentric circles round him. Are not the very hairs of our heads numbered? Is it not the will of our Father that not one of these little ones should perish? Is not egoism bursting into songs like "That will be glory for me" the essential nature of Christianity?

It is amazing to find this flaccid interpretation of a faith whose symbol is the austere Cross. No one would be so astonished as Jesus himself at this rendering of his religion. He did believe in the sacredness of every personality, but to that truth he gave a self-renouncing turn. To give his life for the liberation and elevation of personality, asking as little as possible for himself and expending as much as possible of himself—to Jesus that was the upshot of believing that personality is sacred.

Indeed, as one listens to these Freudians and their various allies, one wonders why, if they really wish to know what religion is, they do not go to its noblest exhibitions. Would they judge music by jazz when there is Beethoven or architecture by automobile filling stations when there is Chartres? What the Freudians call religion Jesus of Nazareth called sin. Such religion was one of his first temptations, and the dramatic narrative of his rejection of it is on record. The Tempter took him to the temple top, so runs the story, and there said to him, "If thou be the Son of God, cast thyself down: for it is written, He shall give his angels charge concerning thee: and in their hands they shall bear thee up, lest at any time thou dash thy foot against a stone." That is to say, Jesus was tempted of the devil to have a religion for comfort only. He was allured by the devil toward a religion in which angels would protect him from the consequences of broken law, and from that Satanic suggestion that he practice religion as the Freudians describe it he turned decisively away.

Follow, then, this life that so began its ministry, until it comes to its climax in Gethsemane. Jesus did not want to bear the torture of the Cross; he had seen folk crucified. His prayer, however, was not the egoistic cry of popular religion, "My will be done," but the contrary prayer of self-renunciation. "Not my will, but thine, be done." Is such religion a compensatory device to make life comfortable? Is it a fantasy by which we overlay cruel fact with pleasing fiction? Is it a world of desire to which we escape for easy solace from a ruthless situation?

A man whose religion, conceived in the spirit of self-renunciation, is centered in God, not as a bed to sleep on but as a banner to follow, is not fooling himself.

Moreover, a religious experience that is not deceitful will be one in which a man does not endeavor to escape the actual world but to transform it. To be sure, much nonsense is talked to-day about the psychological devices by which we retreat from life. The very word "escape" in modern psychiatric jargon has an undesirable significance. As a matter of fact, escapes are among the most admirable of our activities. If some of us could not retreat to nature and re-orient ourselves amid her spaces and silences we should be undone. If some of us could not escape from the hurly-burly of our mechanistic age on the magic carpets of music and poetry to live for a while in the mansions of the spirit, we should collapse. If some of us could not retreat to friendship, life would not be worth living. These are "escapes" but they re-establish us and return us to the world not less but better fitted to grapple with reality and throw it.

Suppose, then, that a man does not believe in atheism as the solution of the cosmic problem. Suppose that he is convinced that the cosmos is a law-abiding and progressive system, grounded in intelligence and patterned by a purpose whose deepest reality is revealed in spiritual life. Shall he not retreat to that? To call that in an evil sense a defense-mechanism is to beg the question. If materialism in any of its forms is true, then, to be sure, religion is a deceptive defense-mechanism, and so are most beautiful things in human experience. But if the world really does have spiritual meaning, then such religion is one of those indispensable orientations of the soul in its real environment which steady, strengthen, and transform our lives.

Religion, however, is much more than retreat,

even when retreat is elevated to its noblest terms. Comfort is a strong word—fort, fortress, fortification, fortitude, fortify are its near relatives—and a great religion always has brought and always will bring comfort. But great religion does so not by escaping from the actual world but by supplying faith and courage to transform it.

When, knowing religious biography at its best, one listens to the new strategists putting religion into the same class with drugs and day-dreams as a means of escape from life, patience becomes difficult. To be sure, cheap men have always held a cheap religion. So a Buddhist priest said to a friend of mine: "Religion is a device to bring peace of mind in the midst of conditions as they are." This attitude is not exclusively Buddhist; much contemporaneous Christianity is of the same breed. It is the ultimate heresy, hating which as a travesty on religion, one welcomes Freud and all his kind if they can make the case against it plainer and press the attack upon it more relentlessly. But to call that cheap article real religion is to forget the notable exhibitions of another kind of faith, from some ancient Moses linking his life to the fortunes of a slave people until he liberated them to some modern Grenfell forgetting himself into immortality in Labrador. Such religion is not akin to drugs and day-dreams; it means not escape from but transformation of the actual world.

It will be a sad day for the race if such religion vanishes. I see no likelihood of getting out of atheism the necessary faith and hope for social progress. That pictures the universe as a crazy book in dealing with which we may indeed be scientific, may count the letters and note the method of their arrangement but may not be religious and so read sense and meaning in the whole. The human mind will not forever avoid the consequences of such a world-view if it prevails.

"It cannot be doubted," one of the new psychological assailants writes, "that God has been a necessity to the human race, that He is still a necessity, and will long continue to be." Indeed he will, and it is notable that even those who think him an illusion admit the fact. Religion has been described as mere superstition, a left-over from the age of magic, a deliberate device of priestcraft for controlling the masses, but to-day such external descriptions are outmoded. Whatever else may be true of it, religion is one of the most deep-seated responses of the human organism, part and parcel of personality's method of getting on in the world. To dismiss it as a branch of pathological psychology is too cavalier a method of disposing of a profound matter.

The Freudians, in this regard, are lifting their sails into a passing gust of wind. Often clouded by ignorance and wandering in uncertainty, using fantasy when fact gives out and mistaking wishes for reality, religion shares the common fate of all things human, but at its heart even the skeptic must at times suspect that it is dealing with truth—"no transient brush of a fancied angel's wing," as Martineau put it, "but the abiding presence and persuasion of the Soul of Souls."

But Religion Is an Art

O NE of the most fascinating movements afoot in religion to-day is the renaissance of interest in beauty. For a long time now religion has been so absorbed in adjusting itself to science and to the new social life created by its inventions that conscious concern about beauty has been practically nil. Every generation tends to have some dominant idea which subjects all others to itself—holds, as it were, a pistol to the head of every aspirant for attention, and asks one categorical question. In thirteenth-century Florence one would expect to hear on every side, "Is it artistically excellent?" or in Russia to-day, "Is it orthodox Communism?" There can be no doubt what question has been pointed at the head of the Western world in these recent generations: "Is it scientific?"

The century from 1830 on was lighted in by tallow-dips and out by electricity; rode in on horseback and out in an airplane; came in talking as the

Neanderthal man did and went out using a micro-
phone; commenced with a quill pen and finished
with a linotype; began with hands for labor and
ended with the powers of the universe in harness.
Along with such visible evidences of scientific
achievement has grown up a new set of ideas, so
demonstrable and so effective both for theoretical
explanation and practical consequence that everything is being tested by them. As a result one per-
emptory challenge now brings all our thinking to
heel: "Is it scientific?"

No area of human life has been more deeply affected by this question than religion. The men of
faith might claim for their positions ancient tradition, practical usefulness, and spiritual desirability;
but one query could prick all such bubbles: "Is it
scientific?" That question has searched religion for
contraband goods, stripped it of old superstitions,
forced it to change its categories of thought and
methods of work, and in general has so thoroughly
cowed and scared religion that many modern-
minded believers, acting like frightened citizens of
New York and Chicago, instinctively throw up
their hands at the mere whisper of it.

The result is that many modernists are desperately
trying to reduce their religion to its scientific elements. Some preachers even trim their language to

scientific terms, and endeavor to talk about the eternal spiritual values as though they were reporting laboratory experiments, or debating Einstein's relativity. Whenever a prominent scientist comes out strongly for religion all the churches thank heaven and take courage as though it were the highest possible compliment to God to have Eddington believe in him. Science has become the arbiter of this generation's thought, until to call even a prophet and a seer scientific is to cap the climax of praise.

The service rendered to religion by this ruthless application of the new categories is incalculable. Not only in detail have great doctrines, like the reign of law, and revolutionary facts, like the new astronomy and evolution, calcined old fables and cleaned up a mess of rubbish in religious tradition; the whole method of science, its scrupulous care for facts, its painstaking, impersonal, objective insistence on getting at facts and their implications, has been inestimably beneficial. Beyond all computation, science has improved the moral tone of religion.

When all this is freely conceded, however, it still remains true that the loveliest things in human experience are not adequately covered by the word "scientific." We have been hoodwinked and hypnotized by the prevalent insistence that everything must be subsumed under this one category, whereas art, music, poetry, love, religion can never be crowded within its limits. They belong as well to the realm of beauty. That realm has standing in its own right; and religion, in its central meanings, is far nearer to being a fine art than to being a science.

To be sure, all realms have somewhere an aspect on which science can speak with authority. Helmholtz, the German physicist, published a learned book in which he explained exactly what different lengths of sound waves and vibrations per second are necessary to produce tones of varied pitch and quality. It is an erudite, scientific treatise on music, which one could learn by heart and accurately comprehend without understanding music in the least. For, while music *has* a scientific aspect, it *is* an art. Its scientific tangencies are important; in a way they are even basic; but they are not central. Music is Palestrina, Bach, Beethoven; it is Toscanini, Kreisler, Gabrilówitsch; it is the soul of man rising up to create beauty through sound; and when one enters into music as an art one finds a range of experience far wider than science can describe, explain, or understand.

Few things that concern either art or religion need more to be said than this. We have been so bulldozed by the question, "Is it scientific?" that, as Paderewski has lately been complaining, "this age is not propitious for art." "There are fewer poets and fewer musicians," he says. "Those who would come in contact with art are obliged to live on what the great masters of the past left us." Important as the service of science has been, the persistent pressing of the question, "Is it scientific?" into every realm has depleted our living; and our hard-headed factual thinking, with its hard-headed and often hard-hearted factual results in a highly mechanized and commercialized civilization, is proving to be starvation diet. In consequence, many like Paderewski feed their souls by going back to unscientific generations where men were asking the towering question, "Is it beautiful?"

No wonder, then, that wide areas of religion are reactionary, that Roman Catholicism has irresistible allurement for minds like Hilaire Belloc and Chesterton, and that religious modernism is often as noisy and thin as jazz! Religion reduced to its scientific elements is as desiccated as the Fifth Symphony reduced to the mathematical formulæ of its sound waves. Religion is nothing if it is not beautiful; and much old religion, knowing nothing of science, did at least understand beauty, clothe itself in external loveliness and often make lovely lives. No religion which forgets that has earned its right to survive. Even life itself is not so much a science as an art, a very difficult and at its best a very fine art, and religious living is no exception.

II

Protestantism, in particular, needs to take this fact to heart, for unhappily the dominance of scientific categories, of which we have been speaking, has only accentuated a tendency already afoot in the historic Protestant tradition. Beautiful buildings, music, rituals, stained glass, festivals, and processions were close to the heart of the old Catholicism; but the Protestant Reformation, distrusting them, at its worst stripped them off as though they were the unclean garments of the Scarlet Woman. Some of us remember rumors of great grandsires who would not keep Christmas—it was Papist. They would not celebrate even Easter—it was Papist. Of such were the iconoclasts, who smashed images, stripped the cathedrals, stopped the holidays, made churches plain and worship bare. To be sure, the love of beauty is too imperious to be utterly repressed, and many a Puritan church, austere as it is, is delectable; yet there is no mistaking the underlying Protestant distrust of beauty in religion.

Of the three realms of spiritual value,—truth, goodness, and beauty,—Protestantism has specialized in the first two and has neglected the third. She has been strong for the true, and has expressed it by dogmatic insistence on doctrine. She has been strong for the good, and has borne down heavily on duty. Doctrine to be believed, duty to be done—that is good Protestantism. But she has had no commensurate interest in the beautiful.

The most obvious illustration of this fact is the hideous, degenerate ecclesiastical architecture of this country. For its worst exhibitions—unpainted wooden boxes, set in unlandscaped lots, presenting within or without hardly a single item to relieve the uniform ugliness—poverty may be a partial excuse. But there is no excuse for the expensive horror of hundreds of our churches with their amphitheatrical arrangement, sloping floors, high platforms, with a man on a red plush chair as the center of attention, a speaker's desk in front of him and painted organ pipes behind. Such churches may be fit to proclaim doctrine and duty in, but they are not conducive to worship; and anyone who goes out from them cleansed and uplifted by a vision of the beautiful has triumphed in imagination over an adverse environment.

To-day Protestants, although for generations inured to such ecclesiastical ugliness, are beginning to rebel. They cannot stand their æsthetic starvation. On every side one feels a rising impatience with glorified lecture halls, sermon-ridden Sunday mornings in which worship is only "opening exercises," trashy hymns, anthems bawled from under the latest millinery, and casual prayers through which the minister strolls into the presence of the Almighty with indecent carelessness. There is an insistent demand that, if we are to worship at all, we do it beautifully, for beauty subdues, integrates, and unifies the soul, washes the spirit clean, and sends one out with a vision of the Divine, not simply believed in but made vivid. We are discovering once more that nothing in human life, least of all religion, is ever right until it is beautiful.

III

This truth as applied to religion, however, goes far beyond the externals of architecture and worship into the very essentials of religious thought and life. Liberal Christians, alike inheriting the old Protestant neglect of beauty and absorbing the new scientific attitude, have been doubly tempted to forget this. If religion seems to be losing ground to-day, one reason is that so many religionists, desperately anxious to validate their position, are absorbed in efforts to prove religion scientific. One might almost as well defend the "Ode to a Nightingale" on the major ground that Keats is scientifically accurate in his ornithology. Let us hope he is accurate; there is no reason why he should not be; beauty and science ideally need not conflict; but if he were as mistaken in details about the nightingale as he was in putting Cortez instead of Balboa on that "peak in Darien" his ode would still be beautiful.

So religion should certainly try not to be unscientific, but the vital meaning of religion is in another realm. For example, religion does not naturally speak the language of science at all. Some doughty propagandists of the faith, trying to run Jesus into modern molds to save his credit in a scientific age, have endeavored to show that, after all, he was very scientifically minded. Upon the contrary, he was not in the least that; he was an artist rather, and used artistic speech. "The kingdom of heaven is like unto," he began, and then he sketched a drama, told a story, drew a picture. A boy leaves home, a widow pleads with an unjust judge, improvident attendants come late to a wedding, flowers are more gorgeously arrayed than Solomon in all his glory—the media of his thought and the vehicles of his expression were dramatic, poetical, symbolic, picturesque. That is, he spoke the native language of religion, which always at its best is the language not of science, but of art.

So tyrannical are scientific categories in our time that to say this about Jesus lowers the estimate of him in many minds. Just so! they think; Jesus was not scientific; he merely used artistic speech. So stupid a judgment is one of the penalties we pay for our lopsided minds. The plain fact is that the language of science changes beyond recognition from one generation to another. If Jesus had used the jargon of his day's scientific speech he would have been utterly forgotten. If we can comprehend him at all it is because he did use the language of beauty, for that alone has timelessness and universality. "All things change: art alone endures."

Ancient Greece is fallen, her armies and empires, business and politics, her science even, marvelous as it was, long gone now and far overpassed. What is left of Homer, however, of Æschylus, Sophocles and Euripides, of Phidias and Praxiteles, of the prose poetry of Plato, is still among our priceless treasures, and we would sacrifice much to find more. Only what Greece put into the language of beauty is assured of permanence.

No folly of religion, therefore, could be more ruinous than the endeavor to jam itself within the categories and vocabulary of contemporary science. What religion most wants to say must be put into artistic vehicles. When religion speaks freely its native tongue it says that the Eternal Spirit is most like a father and that we should live like brethren; that deep within us are spiritual resources like wells, whereof if a man drink he will never thirst again; that behind the race is an Eternal Purpose, like the hills from which our help comes, and ahead of us hope, like a sun forever rising and never going down; that life need not be ugly like a boy feeding husks to swine, but can find its spiritual home; that "strength and beauty are in his sanctuary."

This obviously is not scientific language. Like Paderewski, the man of religion often finds that in using it he is speaking a tongue not tuned to a scientific age. Men talk to him like the woman who once said to Turner that she had never seen such effects in nature as he painted, to whom Turner gave the inevitable answer, "Madam, don't you wish you had?" Yet, in the end, as always, beauty will prove to be timeless and when Einstein is as outmoded as Ptolemy this native speech of religion will still be the language of the soul.

IV

One protest inevitably to be made against such a statement is obvious. This emphasis upon the artistic elements in religion, someone is sure to say, plays directly into the hands of those who claim that religion is altogether subjective, that no objective cosmic reality corresponds with our similes, that, like poetry, religion is loveliness which we ourselves create and is not at all a report on the truth about the universe. To be sure, the protester says, religion may be just as beautiful as we have art enough to make it, but so far from being true to cosmic fact, it is subjective finery hung like a tapestry to cover the bare, stark walls of a ruthless world.

Once more, in this familiar protest, we see our generation being hypnotized into believing that only the scientific report of the cosmos represents the truth. To a religious mind, however, eagerly accepting that report but refusing hypnosis, it seems clear that a scientific description never tells the whole truth about anything; it gives only a partial, abstracted aspect of the truth. John Smith may properly be listed in the telephone book as Riverside 2693, and one may gladly accept this as a valuable piece of information, but it would be sheer bulldozing to endeavor to persuade us that it tells the whole truth about Smith. So, from the scientific description of a symphony in terms of its counted air-waves to the pointer readings of modern astrophysics, science gives us a description of reality which, however accurate and marvelous, covers only part of the truth.

Water is more than H_2O. Water is rainbows and

cataracts, dew and stormy seas; Tennyson's brook and Byron's "deep and dark blue Ocean" are water; and no strictly scientific description deals adequately with that rich and varied totality of which hydrogen and oxygen are the measurable base.

The point at issue here is crucial, not only for religion but for art. Art at its highest has insisted that it was not simply beautiful but was also telling the truth. Take from the supreme artists in any realm the conviction that their beauty is the fruit of genuine vision, that they are seeing and reporting something eternally true, and their art will be despoiled. Great art, like great religion, never has surrendered to the idea that it is subjective only; it always has been convinced that no one can know the whole of reality without seeing what the artist sees.

Science runs headlong into conflict with both art and religion, therefore, not in its special doctrines—only obscurantists are permanently troubled by them—but in its exponents who claim an absolute monopoly of all paths to truth. An automobile road-map of the Barbizon country may be scientifically exact; but no one could hypnotize Corot into believing that the picture which he painted of a Barbizon roadway was not also true. His would be another aspect of the truth phrased in a vehicle of expression that could not properly be called either scientific or unscientific, but it would be true—to some of us, if we had to choose, the more important part of the truth. In denying monopoly to scientific categories, therefore, the artist has as much at stake as the religionist, as Shelley clearly saw when, not in the name of religion but of poetry, he vehemently protested against the new obsession that the heights of truth can be reached by any "owl-winged faculty of calculation."

At this point, Elmer Davis, for example, in a vigorous, fine-spirited essay on "God Without Religion," seems to me to miss the mark. He takes Eddington to task for superimposing on his scientific world-view another way of getting at reality —the mystic route of insight and intuition. Now, Davis is entirely at liberty to raise serious question as to Eddington's mysticism and its unverifiable subjectiveness, but Davis really ought to take more seriously than he does what Eddington is driving at. Like many another who knows science thoroughly, Eddington is convinced that when everything in the universe reachable by the scientific method has been discovered a large part of the universe has not been reached at all. We may dispute with him his way of putting this matter, but the matter itself still remains—his basic certainty, namely, that we can no more exhaust reality by scientific pointer readings than we could exhaust the Sistine Madonna by a chemical analysis of its paint. Nor will it do to toss this extrascientific remainder aside as merely subjective. The beauty of the Sistine Madonna is not so accurately verifiable but it is objective, as the chemical analysis is; neither of them can be got at without the operation of mind but both are there, genuinely discovered and not subjectively concocted by either analyst or appreciator. It is inadequate dealing to call that overplus, in picture or in universe at large, mere intuition, and to dispose of it with a wisecrack that when it comes to intuition "every man must roll his own."

Nor does Davis fare better, so it seems to me, when, thus disposing of the extrascientific realm of spiritual values, he faces the necessity of explaining how that realm came to be in our experience at all —so much the noblest thing in us, the essence of whatever dignity our human nature has. He is too clear-headed not to see that the nub of his problem lies at that point, and too straightforward not to say frankly what his position forces him to think. The telltale sentences inevitably, though I should guess reluctantly, are written consenting to the idea that life may be merely "a disease which afflicts matter in its old age." Which is to say, in effect, that human life with its rich and growing experience of spiritual values is an utterly fortuitous affair:

that at one stage in the planet's cooling the heat happened to be just right, and from that unique befalling of chemical good fortune life emerged, and out of life personality, and out of personality the world of values which we know as art, music, poetry, knowledge, love, religion. Behind everything spiritually valuable, then, from a laughing child to a table of logarithms, from Joachim's Hungarian Concerto to the character of Christ, the original, primary, causative factor, then, is simply the fact that once, while the planet cooled, the heat happened to be right. I maintain that to believe that is to believe in magic, and that the chance of its being true, as Professor Montague of Columbia says, would be represented by a fraction with the numerator 1 and a denominator that would reach from here to one of the fixed stars. Indeed the wildest devotees of magic in history never got much farther away than that from serious dealing with the law of adequate causation.

When, therefore, we see the central meanings of religion in terms of art rather than of science, it does not mean that we are careless about truth. We seriously think that the realm of spiritual values is a revelation of something eternally so. Great art itself never is careless about truth. It is part of our present scientific obsession that on one side our generation thinks of art as mere prettiness, and on the other interprets it in terms of pictures which take prizes when hung upside down. The supreme artists, however, have always thought that they were the supreme truth-tellers. They have regarded as incredible the supposition that the language of metric description can compass reality. Like Shelley, impatient of conventional religion, they may write themselves down "atheist," but like Shelley too, believing in

That Beauty in which all things work and move,

they have, at their best, thought that the spiritual values which they have seen and loved have a cosmic meaning, that artistry is really in the structure of the universe, and that their insights are a report on something everlastingly so.

V

Though religion is interested in truth, then, often with a fierceness that science cannot surpass, it is interested rather as art is; and in a scientific age this leads to all sorts of misunderstanding. Harry Elmer Barnes, for example, with good-natured lustiness, has recently been laying out the devotees of the "Jesus stereotype." He sees the danger of trying to solve modern problems by appeal to a first-century Palestinian, whose conditioning environment and ways of thought were utterly incommensurate with present needs. He wants the conscience of today free to operate without that ancient stencil through which so often Christians merely paint over a present moral issue with the name of Christ. In all this Barnes is saying something that Christians ought to heed. There is a deal of dodging in the churches, where a text from Jesus or a vague appeal to his personality is made to do duty for the serious facing of contemporaneous questions. But the man of religion never would agree that the solution of that problem is to withdraw our devotion from Jesus.

The underlying difficulty with Barnes and his like is simply that they are scientifically minded, and that no science ever treats its creative personalities as religion treats Jesus, Buddha, and other founders of religions. Science abstracts from Copernicus the ideas of Copernicus, keeps such as remain valid, throws the residue away, and leaves the matter there. Copernicus, the individual, science does not adore. Barnes is really telling us to treat Christ like that, to take the few permanently valid and basic ideas of his thinking, forget the rest, let his personality sink into ancient history, and move on. All of which shows that, while men like Barnes may understand science, they do not understand art or religion.

It is entirely possible to abstract Copernicus' scientific ideas from Copernicus, but no one can abstract Toscanini's art from Toscanini. Toscanini's art *is* Toscanini.

When we move over from science to art we pass from the realm of general and abstract propositions to the realm of creative personal values, which, far from being general and abstract, are intensely individual. Put a dozen scientists at work on the same problem and, if they are accurate, they will get a dozen identical results. Give a dozen artists the same task, let us say to paint a Madonna, and we shall happily get a dozen different results. This does not mean that the artist's work is whimsically intuitional and merely subjective; the spiritual values, and even the historical setting which they are painting, are as objective as the laws of nature; but it does mean that while science works for a general and abstract formula, art works for an individual, differential beauty.

When we study even sonnets scientifically, we get the laws that cover all sonnets; when we turn to sonnets artistically, we fall in love with some special sonnet like Milton's "On His Blindness." When we study love scientifically, we seek the physical and psychological factors that enter into all love; when we think of love artistically, we turn to some special love like Elizabeth Barrett's for Robert Browning. While, therefore, for the purposes of science one can reduce Copernicus to Copernicus' ideas, when Rodin, the French sculptor, talks of his art he rises into rapture about Phidias and says that he never can be surpassed.

Religion, then, being always at its center closer to art than to science, will only ruin itself if it takes Barnes and his like too seriously on the "Jesus stereotype." We may well learn from such honest and able critics to shun the misuses of Jesus, which he himself would be the first to condemn; but to abstract Jesus' religion from Jesus is to make a cold formula out of a vivid personality. So William James, when asked once to define spirituality, hesitated and finally said that he was not sure that he could define the quality but he could point out a spiritual personality—Phillips Brooks. William James understood religion; he knew its native speech. It never wins the world by general propositions but by concrete embodiments of spiritual beauty. It knows that Jesus' religion is Jesus. This should no more enslave us to a "stereotype" than Rodin's admiration of Phidias enslaved him or even lessened his exuberant originality, but whether religion uses this method of procedure well or ill it inevitably uses it. It thinks in symbols of concrete personal life.

VI

This symbolism of art and religion leads point-blank to one of the chief difficulties that a scientific age has with both of them—their vagueness. Science is all for accuracy; its measures must be exact, its terms clipped and concise, its definitions meticulous, its propositions demonstrable. With such metric exactitude as the beau ideal of procedure, a prevalent type of scientific mind turns to religion or art and finds itself in a strange land. Here men are using similes and metaphors, are adumbrating truths they cannot define and capturing in symbols fugitive glimpses of realities which forever elude their understanding. It is no wonder that in an age obsessed by science art and religion face an uncongenial climate.

Nevertheless, religion and art will make the mistake of their long existence if they capitulate. Even science to-day all along the line is sacrificing definiteness to get at truth. Physics, which a few years ago was dealing with little, hard, round, solid atoms, is now dealing with "fields of force"—losing somewhat in clarity of outline and gaining much in adequacy of statement. Astrophysics, also, which hardly a few months ago was using absolute measuring rods, is now telling us that a yardstick's length is relative to the speed with which it is traveling through space and, to the mental horror of us mid-Victorians, advanced scientists are bringing back chance into their world-view and teaching that the once rigid laws of nature are merely approximations of statistical averages. The new science itself is likely to be the death of those little minds which lately have been rolling the cosmos into a formula and swallowing it. Our new knowledge is getting out into depths where vagueness is difficult to avoid and where, as Jeans says, "The ultimate realities of the universe are at present quite beyond the reach of science, and may be—and probably are—forever beyond the comprehension of the human mind."

Now, art and religion always have known that these rigid definitions of reality are insufficient. They have always known that adequate thinking must have fringes, and that when the deepest truths are to be spoken only a symbol can do it. To be sure, religion has often sinned against its best nature, trying to beat science at its own game, and defining God, as Leslie Stephen put it, with an accuracy that modest naturalists would shrink from in describing the genesis of a black beetle. But such theological dogmatism has nearly been the death of religion, and only by outgrowing its strangling constrictions has religion managed to survive.

By all means, let a man in his religious thinking be as clear-headed and precise as possible, but let him remember that even Einstein, dealing with a metric matter and having mathematics for his language, resorts at last to the approximation of a picture, and says that "Space now is turning around and eating up matter." Much more, then, religion, dealing not so much with things as with values, must go beyond its definitions, and, like art, speak its truest word in a simile.

In *A Preface to Morals* Walter Lippmann lets fly this: "No painter who ever lived could make a picture which expressed the religion of the Rev. Harry Emerson Fosdick." As a matter of fact, the real trouble with the school of thought to which I belong is that often one cannot make much of anything out of its religion *except* a picture. We probably are not theological enough, have artistic rather than philosophic minds; we are immensely interested, indeed, in attempted definitions in religious theory, but have the less confidence in them the more precise they are; and, when we say what religion really means to us, we talk in symbols. Strangely enough, Walter Lippmann's criticism applies less to us than to himself. He says with repeated

iteration throughout his book that the essence of
his religion is "disinterestedness." May I suggest
that some day he try persuading an artist to paint
a picture of *that*?

As for us, a definition of God seems an absurd
thing to ask. We have no definition of God—"*Dieu
défini est Dieu fini*"; we have only a roadway that
leads out toward God. We are convinced beyond
peradventure that he who travels merely the path of
electrons, atoms, molecules toward a vision of the
Ultimate misses it, and that he who travels the
road of spiritual values—goodness, truth, beauty—
finds it. The eternal and creative Power cannot be
adequately approached through the metrical world
alone; the innermost nature of the Ultimate is revealed also in the personal world of spiritual values
—of that we are confident. When, however, we talk
about God so approached, trying to utter what lies
at the end of the roadway the beginning of which
alone is within our reach, we have only symbols
for our speech. Now, as always, they are the native
language of religion. God is like something—a rock,
a fortress, a high tower, a father or a friend, a
Buddha or a Christ.

That this process is full of danger is obvious.
Many who use the symbols of religion do not know
what they are doing. They read poetry as prose, take

similes with deadly literalness, make a dogma from a metaphor. They call God a person, and to hear them do it one would think that our psychological processes could naïvely be attributed to the Eternal. It is another matter altogether, understanding symbolic language, to call God personal when one means that up the roadway of goodness, truth, and beauty, which outside personal experience have no significance, one must travel toward the truth about the Ultimate—"beyond the comprehension of the human mind." Of course, that is vague; no idea of the Eternal which is not vague can possibly approximate the truth.

I confess, then, that when a man like Walter Lippmann, hearing God interpreted in terms of spiritual values, exclaims, "But certainly this is not the God of the ancient faith. This is not God the Father, the Lawgiver, the Judge. This is a highly sophisticated idea of God," I am dumfounded. Would he say that, because the pointer readings of modern astrophysics which Eddington insists are merely symbols of the truth are immensely more recondite and elusive than the old flat and stationary earth, there is, therefore, no truth in them and we must keep the old flat earth or else give up the cosmic problem altogether? Yet what Lippmann says about God is precisely as sensible as that. Of course, the approach to God in this new universe does not give us the pictures of God belonging to 1000 B.C. or even 1000 A.D. Of course, the hard outlines of old definitions have given way to ideas much more comprehensive and much less rigid. But this ultimately means neither intellectual vacuity nor spiritual loss. As well tell Eddington to get back to the flat earth or else surrender cosmology altogether. What we have in the new approach to God is the conviction, immeasurably sustaining and enriching to life, that this cosmos, which created personal spiritual values and sustains them, cannot be adequately interpreted without reference to them, and that the road which leads out to the truth about God begins in the goodness and beauty that we know.

That men like Davis and Lippmann, however, have just ground for protest at this point is clear. They charge us, who thus interpret the Eternal in the symbols of beauty, with conveniently forgetting that the world is also full of ugliness.

> "Our rainbow arch, Thy mercy's sign,
> All, save the clouds of sin, are Thine, "

sings Oliver Wendell Holmes. Well, as a young woman once wrote me after hearing this hymn in a church service, this is letting God off altogether too easily. No honest religion can so hide behind its symbols of beauty as to forget the dual nature of the world. Righteousness and rottenness, fine homes and insane asylums, glorious creative work and unemployment, the laughter of children and three hundred burned to death in a prison, forget-me-nots and earthquakes—it's a queer business. From "the beauty and the terror of the world," as Stevenson called it, to pick out the rainbows as symbols of the Eternal and forget the clouds of ugliness and sin will never do.

While, however, I deeply sympathize with Davis on this point and, like himself, often feel baffled in trying to perceive goodness at the heart of creation, I do not see that, even intellectually speaking, he is in any better case. He sees so much evil in the cosmos that he thinks man is the sole possessor of all the goodness there is, and is persuaded that in the fight for the progress of goodness there is no conspirator beyond ourselves. That is, he surrenders to ugliness as we religionists do to beauty. He puts *that* into the center of his picture of the cosmos, makes that creative and beauty fortuitous. *Tu quoque!* We are all in the same boat in this mysterious world. In the long run if we think about the cosmos at all, we surrender either to its beauty or its ugliness, making one basic and the other ephemeral. Theists and non-theists alike, we all are artists; none of us has a formula that touches bottom; we have only pictures. Some of us choose as symbols of the Ultimate a ruthless, purposeless mechanism, producing ugliness by its very nature and casual beauty by accident, and some of us choose the artistry of the cosmos, its law-abiding, regular procedures, its emergent evolution of higher structures, its personalities at last with spiritual life, creative power, and social progress, as the significant revelatory facts. Nor is this choice a whimsy, a wish-fulfilment, a throw of volition's dice; it has behind it too great a weight of philosophic opinion from Plato to Whitehead to be treated thus cavalierly. To surrender to the ugliness of the world our cosmic outlook seems to me as irrational as it is disheartening. Doubtless, the final truth takes both the beauty and the terror in and, in that comprehensive view which no human mind is large enough to grasp, I am confident that the secondary element will not be beauty.

VII

The most serious peril in this modern renaissance of beauty is moral. Æsthetic sensibility has always been used by some as a place of retreat from ethical seriousness. Masson in his life of Milton calls his hero a standing exception to the common rule that poets and artists generally "are and ought to be distinguished by a predominance of sensibility over principle." Let psychologists explain it as they will, it is biographically obvious that the æsthetic and ethical temperaments are commonly disparate and the Miltons who combine them few and far between.

In any age, therefore, when religion becomes consciously a fine art we are likely to see beauty made a substitute for righteousness, with the result that some Puritan reaction will later have its innings. So the Greek Church under the Tsars, largely shut out from ethical expression in social life, created the most gorgeous ceremonials and the most moving religious music of the Christian Church.

Of course, art deeply understood is not thus aloof from life but itself takes life with consuming seriousness. Music approached as a theory or a diversion may make the dilettante, but music approached as an art is fearfully demanding. The devotee must take time, practice, acquire technic, achieve skill, and in so doing make sacrifices that would put most moralists to shame.

Whether the æsthetic approach to religion can be made thus ethically earnest is a crucial problem in certain areas of churchmanship to-day. Our present civilization is too inhuman and unhappy to be much helped by a religion which provides in beauty a mere escape from moral problems. A religion which does not build dependable personal integrity, which does not assist in clearing up our profoundly immoral economic situation and our international difficulties, where war is as insane as it is wicked, cannot by any æsthetic appeal make up for its ethical failure. That, however, is a problem by itself.

The inadequacy of this argument most likely to call out protest is, I should suppose, its injustice to science. For while it is possible, as we have done, to distinguish the attitudes of science and art and set them down in contrast, the resultant statement does not represent the actual experience of scientists. To them science also is beautiful. In the picture of the cosmos to which it leads, in the delicacy of its measurements and the marvel of its disclosures, in the ventures of imagination by which it pushes out its hypotheses, science is beautiful. Moreover, all science is crowned in art, as medicine is fulfilled in the art of the physician's practice, anatomy in the surgeon's skill, psychology in education and psychiatry, sociology in measures of reform, electricity in illumination, and in the art of flying more sciences than one can count. Even the humdrum commercialized results of science take on artistic forms, so that railroad stations, once grossly utilitarian, are now made as monumental as possible, skyscrapers, once eyesores, are now an emergent order of new architecture, and, with the coming of giant power, the hope rises of cities freed from present ugliness and made lovely to live in. For science, as for all the rest of man's experience, artistic expression is the crown of life, and nothing is right until it is beautiful.

Unless some new *débâcle* of human folly, like the Great War, wrecks our chance, we are moving out into a renaissance of beauty all along our civilization's line. Undoubtedly religion feels the stir and recognizes in it the opportunity to reclaim some of its lost heritage. It may use the opportunity merely to bring in a new day of ceremonial pomp and circumstance, with processionals substituted for convictions and sacraments for moral seriousness, or it may succeed in making beauty for multitudes an allurement to goodness and a pathway to God.

Morals Secede from the Union

LISTENING to current discussion one would suppose that the future of religion were being decided on the scientific front, but a far more critical battle is being waged on the ethical front, where morals are denying that they need religion and are seceding from the union.

As far back as history goes, morals and religion have been mingled. Among primitive people right conduct was any kind of behavior which secured the favor of the tribal gods, and sin was action of any sort—whether, as in David's case, it was lust for Bathsheba or taking a census—which roused a god's antipathy. The basic business of life, therefore, was to know the divine likes and dislikes; and the baffling moral muddle then sprang from the fact that the whims of the deities were dubious.

From that day to this, in one way or another, morals and religion have remained entangled, even in utilitarian schools of ethics which might theoretically have dispensed with the alliance. When, therefore, morals issue their declaration of independence, announcing that neither the definitions nor sanctions of right conduct need religion, revolution is afoot.

That the age-long ideas of morality's dependence on religion have collapsed is obvious. For example, morals historically have relied on supernatural rewards and punishments. A modern preacher might fairly envy the ancient pulpiteers. Believing in supernaturalism, and sure that when God was sufficiently angered by man's sin he would reach forth the besom of his wrath and sweep his enemies away, they used the fear of God dreadfully. So Savonarola shook Florence. So when a comet hung over Boston, Increase Mather paralyzed his congregation: "The Lord hath fired his beacon in the heavens among the stars of God there. . . . The warning piece of heaven is going off."

Projected into the next world, supernatural sanctions of morality became even more terrific. Half a century ago many American children were reared on three books of Bible stories: *Line upon Line*, and *Precept upon Precept*, covering the Old Testament, and *The Peep of Day*, covering the New. Around that last book had gathered in my imagination a halo of happy reminiscence until recently I read some of it quoted as follows:

> At last Jesus will sit upon a white throne, and everybody will stand round his throne. He will open some books, in which he has written down all the naughty things people have done. God has seen all the naughty things you have done. He can see in the dark as well as in the light, and knows all your naughty thoughts. . . .
>
> This is what God will do to those who do not love him. God will bind them in chains and put them in a lake of fire. There they will gnash their teeth and weep and wail forever. . . . They shall not have one drop of water to cool their burning tongues.

I had often wondered why, with my wholesome family life, I had suffered, when but a child, such a devastating horror of hell. Now I know—*The Peep of Day* did it!

Moreover, morals have depended on the supernatural dictation of ethical codes. When one reviews the story, even in recent times, of the entanglement of morals with an inspired Bible, from the endeavors in Calvin's Geneva or in the Massachusetts Bay Colony to base whole commonwealths on Biblical prescription, through scriptural defenses of religious persecution, slavery, and war, to meticulous Sabbath observance on the basis of the Hebrew code, one wonders that such a snarl should ever come undone. Undoubtedly, however, the whole idea of supernatural dictation has petered out. "Thou shalt not commit adultery" seems to many of us excellent morals. This generation, however, will walk around the idea, look it over, size it up, watch its consequences, listen to anyone from Bertrand Russell to Bishop Manning, and decide; but one thing this generation will not do is to accept even that command on supernatural authority.

II

The secession of morals from their historic union with religion, however, is much more thoroughgoing than the mere denial of supernal codes and sanctions. Many religious personalities, both ancient and modern, have not loved goodness because its rules were divinely dictated or because rewards and punishments were divinely administered; they have sought the good life for its own sake, as an artist loves beauty, for no reasons extraneous to its own excellence. Nevertheless, through their goodness they have moved to their idea of the Divine. Thinking of God they have thought of good, and thinking of good they have thought of God, until, like light and heat in sunshine, the two have seemed to them one thing.

To-day, however, we are told that in this amalgam the basic element is morals and that religious faith is only the shadow which earthly ideas of goodness, developed out of human relationships, have cast upon the sky.

> By all that He requires of me,
> I know what God himself must be,

Whittier sings, and inadvertently reveals the true chronology of ethics and religion. First, from practical earthly experience we discover what is good and then we imagine back of the cosmos a Figure whose goodness is like our own. Neither our initial ideas of goodness, they say, nor our motives for achieving it, came from the Figure; he is a shadow, and when the shadow vanishes nothing serious has happened to the good life itself. That was here first. "An honest God is the noblest work of man."

Old theological controversies and Biblical fundamentalisms—"the credibility of Genesis and the edibility of Jonah"—no longer bother intelligent religious men, but this secession of morals from religion would better bother them. We hardly have grown accustomed in other fields to the discovery that science, not religion, supplies the method for meeting most of our urgent needs. The old universe, built like a duplex apartment, where man stood on the ground floor and cried upstairs for gifts to be sent down to him, has gone, and many things our fathers sought from God we get by fulfilling law-abiding conditions. Still, at one point the need of religion has seemed impregnable: it has been indispensably entangled with the motives and sanctions of the good life. With God regarded as an afterthought, however, neither creative of the good nor necessary to sustain it, we are advised to cease worrying about theism and to give up asking whether the universe has moral purpose at the heart of it. There may be no cosmic purpose, but there are many good purposes on earth for which to live. There may be no good God, but all the goodness still is left from which our ideas of the good God were derived.

If religion is no longer necessary either to get the things which we desire or to achieve the moral goals toward which we aspire, of what use is it, anyway? Why not let morals secede from the union without a struggle?

III

An initial doubt of successful secession is suggested by the fact that there seems to be a native kinship between atheism and discouragement. However one approaches the matter, that kinship appears.

We commonly are told that faith in God can be psychologically explained; it is a cosmic projection of our wishes, a rationalization of our emotional needs and hopes. But, by the same sign, disbelief in God is also open to psychological accounting; it is the cosmic projection of our sense of life's futility, the rationalization of bafflement, aimlessness, and failure.

After dealing in intimate conference for many years with all varieties of theists and atheists, I venture the generalization that very little atheism springs merely or mainly from skeptical philosophy. For the most part it is emotionally caused. It translates into terms of a Godless, purposeless, ruthless world an inner experience of grief, frustration, or fear, or, as in Russia, it is the theoretical echo of practical resentments and revulsions. A typical woman, for example, sought help in her atheism. Before she had talked three minutes the counselor stopped her with the request that she cease telling about her philosophy and begin on her love-affair. To her surprised protest he said: "To be sure, I am guessing. You may have had some other form of emotional devastation. Without intending it, however, you have unmistakably revealed that you got into your atheism, not by the philosophical, but by the emotional route. Something is going wrong in your life." Then she collapsed and poured out the story of an emotional catastrophe of which her atheism was only a superficial rationalization.

I happen to know that one of the most popular, persuasive, and ruthless statements of atheism in modern times comes from a man battling with a fatal disease and that this book represents primarily the way he feels about life. So one of George Eliot's characters put it long ago: "I look at it as if the doctrines was like finding names for your feelings."

The idea of the assailants of religion, therefore, that faith in God can be finally disposed of as a rationalization of our wishes, simply will not work. In that regard, theism and atheism are on all fours; we get at both of them by the emotional route, and yet one of them must be true. Some higher court of appeal, some well-argued philosophy, striving cannily to avoid the perverting twists of our subtly rationalizing minds, must decide the issue, so far as intellect can decide it. All that we are driving at here is that atheism is a natural and frequent rationalization of discouragement.

When life is empty, barren, lonely, frustrated, and futile, when the world looks dark and human existence purposeless, atheism already is close at hand. To be sure, at that point one can make a wild escape into the comfort of some compensating idealistic philosophy, but for many the next step is to translate the feeling of a devastated experience into the theory of a godless universe.

If, on the other hand, one approach this kinship between atheism and discouragement from the theoretical end, the fact still appears. Consider, for example, a typical modern like Theodore Dreiser, saying:

I find life to be not only a complete illusion or mirage which changes and so escapes or eludes one at every point, but the most amazing fanfare of purely temporary and always changing and ever vanishing and, in the main, clownish and ever ridiculous interests that it has ever been my lot to witness. . . . At best, whatever man does is something that can only prolong the struggles and worries and for the most part futile dreams of those with whom he finds himself companioned here in this atomic or cellular welter, and which in the last analysis may be just nothing at all—a phantasmagoric or cinematic shadow play. . . . As I see him, the unutterably infinitesimal individual weaves among the mysteries a floss-like and wholly meaningless course—if course it be. In short, I catch no meaning from all I have seen, and pass quite as I came, confused and dismayed.

One would have to psychoanalyze Mr. Dreiser to discover whether his futilism is the result of his atheism or his atheism the cosmic projection of his futilism, but the congeniality between the two is clear.

When, therefore, the claim is made that irreligion need not affect morals, the first answer is at hand:

irreligion seems deeply to affect *morale*, and both etymology and life have stemmed morale and morals from the same root.

This fact is not controverted by any discovery of individual atheists who are exuberant or individual religionists who are depressed. A thousand and one interflowing streams of influence affect temperament and there are all kinds of religion and irreligion. Moreover, many of our contemporary agnostics and atheists were reared in profoundly religious homes and there were trained in practical and emotional responses to life which they will never altogether lose, no matter what theories they adopt. I do not see, however, how anyone acquainted with modern life and literature can avoid observing the constant, consistent, and logical kinship between thorough-going irreligion and lowered enthusiasm about life.

When, for example, George John Romanes, the scientist, temporarily lost his religious faith, he did not forthwith begin to eat, drink, and be merry, for to-morrow he would die. The result was more oblique. "When at times I think, as think at times I must," he wrote, "of the appalling contrast between the hallowed glory of that creed which once was mine, and the lonely mystery of existence as now I find it—at such times I shall ever feel it impossible to avoid the sharpest pang of which my nature is susceptible." The first effect of "the lonely mystery of existence" is not on a man's morality, but on his morale.

The basic fact with which we are dealing here is that, after all, man's life is a unity, and however we may departmentalize him into the economic man, the scientific man, the moral man, the religious man, and declare each realm autonomous, influences do inevitably leak from one compartment to another.

Especially is it true that if a man has any faith about the meaning of the cosmos he cannot keep it from splashing over into his morale. Suppose that a man believes in mind, not matter, as the Creative Power in this universe, thinks God real, believes in a moral purpose running through creation, conceives human personality not as a whimsy of the dust but as a child of the Spirit, and, far from supposing death to be the end, joins in Emerson's confidence,

> . . . What is excellent,
> As God lives, is permanent.

As a plain matter of history, such a response to the whole meaning of life is so towering and influential a fact that it is folly to neglect it.

By the same sign, if a man disbelieves all this, espouses materialism, thinks the universe as a whole purposeless, supposes man to be a chance by-product of the earth without spiritual origin, individual hope beyond death, or even racial perpetuity on a transient planet, that response to the total meaning of life is also a towering and influential fact. And if one wabbles between the two, is confused and bewildered concerning the whole cosmic business, or throws up his hands altogether in despair of thinking anything worth while about it, that response may be even more impelling.

When, therefore, religious people are challenged to be realistic about this matter and to recognize how seldom we consciously appeal to cosmic theories in deciding daily moral choices, the answer seems ready. Realism is precisely the attitude we are driving at, and the upshot of the search is that we find that people's lives get made up as a whole and not in sections. They develop a total reaction to life. They achieve a spiritual climate. We see men like Anatole France, with creative genius, large achievement, hosts of friends, and ample wealth, saying: "There is not in all the universe a creature more unhappy than I. People think me happy. I have never been happy for one day, not for a single hour." What kind of reaction is that, moral or religious? Is it the man's ethics speaking there or his utter skepticism about any spiritual significance in the universe? Realistically it surely is not one or the other, but both. France, like all the rest of us, found that life gets made up one way or another into a total response to the meaning of existence.

After all, morals are not simply paying one's bills, obeying traffic regulations, returning borrowed umbrellas, or anything else that can be indifferently performed in one kind of world as well as in another. Our morals, at their deepest, are our innermost response to life, our spiritual quality, taste, and motive—and that, separated from our total philosophy, is as unreal as the smile abstracted from the face of the cat in *Alice in Wonderland*.

So far from being satisfied, therefore, with the present slogan, Separate morals from religion! we are sure that the need to-day is another slogan altogether: Seek a total attitude toward life that will at once be good religion and good morals!

IV

The truth of what we have been saying is especially evident in the popular futilism which is at once a moral and a religious problem. Our ethical disorder is superficially exhibited in crime waves, economic injustice, corrupt politics, and sexual promiscuity. Permeating all this, however, is the prevalent sense of life's essential meaninglessness and futility. To be sure, only articulate intellectuals get their cynicism verbally expressed, talking with Thomas Hardy about

> . . . the dreaming, dark, dumb Thing
> That turns the handle of this idle Show!

None the less does such futilism run through popular thought and like a change of weather affect the moral flora of the whole countryside.

Many to-day have traveled the complete route from faith to cynicism. They have doubted everything they once believed—church and creed, God and immortality; they have doubted any sense or purpose in the universe or any goal ahead; they have doubted whatever old bases of idealistic living they ever had until they have reached that apogee of disillusionment where man becomes "a small but boisterous bit of the organic scum that for the time being coats part of the surface of one small planet." Then, having through doubt stripped life of serious significance, they begin doubting their doubts. Like the fabled serpent, disbelief turns to eat itself. The complete skeptic at last disbelieves his own disbeliefs; he cannot have faith in his lack of faith. About that time, life as a whole becomes a mess.

Such cynicism profoundly affects morals, but to call it a moral as distinguished from a religious problem is to misunderstand it altogether. Whether or not the futilist is right in his view of life concerns not simply duty, but doctrine. Man may be an accidental ripple inadvertently blown up on the cosmic surface. He may be, on the other hand, a spiritual adventurer in a spiritual world where all the best in him is response to the Eternal Best. To suppose that our ideas of duty, and especially our spirit in performing it, will be unaffected by our drift toward cynical doctrine or its opposite is sheer romancing. Popular futilism to-day is everywhere bedeviling morals, but it is a great deal more than a moral matter; it is a total set of the mind not only about what men *ought to do*, but about what men essentially and cosmically *are*.

Much current talk about morals without religion, dodging this real issue, proceeds upon the incredible assumption that there can be serious discussion of what man ought to be without serious discussion of what man is. *Oughtness*, however, is essentially related to *isness*—even the virtues which an airplane should possess could not be intelligently discussed without knowing what an airplane is—and on that simple fact the endeavor of morals to secede from religion will in the end wreck itself. For while morals deal with what men ought to do and be, religion is basically a message about what men are. They are not the scum of the earth, says a high religion, the accidental by-product of a merely physical cosmos; they are personalities, spiritual beings whose powers of intellection, purposefulness, good will, spring from the nature of the Real World and are necessary to interpret the full truth about it. They are, in a word, sons of God, and it does not yet appear what they shall be. To suppose that morals, dealing with what man ought to be, can blithely wave farewell to this basic problem regarding what men are, that the Ideal for man is unrelated to the Fact about man, is to disregard obvious human experience. As Professor Hocking of Harvard put it on purely psychological grounds, "there is a deep tendency in human nature to *become like* that which we imagine ourselves to be." To persuade all the race, then, to imagine themselves small but boisterous bits of organic scum would make a moral difference in the end; and to persuade men to rally their characters and careers around a high idea of human life as a spiritual adventure in a Spiritual World would make a difference, too. The basic reason why morals never will succeed in seceding from religion is the impossibility of unscrambling *ought* from *is*.

Indeed, "ought" essentially means our sense of the possible resident in the actual and crying out to be fulfilled. Anything we think, therefore, about the nature of the actual affects our faith in the possible. Futilism is a total mind-set about the mean and contemptible nature of the actual, which inevitably falls like a blight on the idea of the possible. In this regard, a man's life as a whole does get made up one way or another, and the consequence is both moral and religious.

To say that a man may have thrown over all the creeds and churches, may have disbelieved every description of God he ever heard, and still may be a first-rate man and a good citizen, is no answer to this contention. That is merely identifying religion with religions, which in this realm is the shortest cut to folly. Let all our present modes of religious thought disappear, the basic fact would still remain: what man ought to be, and may be expected to be, depends on what man is, and what man is is the profoundest moral and religious question in the world.

V

Despite much talk about morals seceding from the union, therefore, I question the success of the independent confederacy. We still shall find ourselves making our total emotional and intellectual response to our situation in this cosmos. Our scientific response will be made in the interest of discovering how we can control our world; our moral response in the interest of discovering how we ought to act in our world; our religious response in the interest of discovering what our world as a whole means. Some, to be sure, will insist that they cannot make up their minds about that last matter—only to discover that they cannot altogether avoid making up their *lives* about it. And those who do make up minds and lives about it in terms of a high confidence that life "means intensely, and means good," will find the whole tone and temper of living affected, its horizons widened, its resources deepened, its hopes quickened, its morale incalculably strengthened.

A religious man's vital conviction concerning the nature of the world he lives in, being as it is an inseparable part of his personal response to life, is germinative, fecund, creative. It raises life's temperature. In a purposeful universe where the Divine experienced in our human values is only the near end of the Divine that fills the cosmos, the weather is different from the prevailing climate, let us say, in George Jean Nathan's world. He writes:

To me pleasure and my own personal happiness—only infrequently collaborating with that of others—are all I deem worth a hoot. . . . As a matter of fact, the happiness and welfare of mankind are not my profession; I am perfectly willing to leave them to the care of the professional missionaries of one sort or another; I have all that I can do to look out for my own happiness and welfare. . . . I am against all reforms and all reformers. The world, as I see it, is sufficiently gay, beautiful and happy as it stands. It is defective only to those who are themselves defective, who lack the sagacity, imagination, humor and wit to squeeze out its rich and jocose juices and go swimming in them. . . . I am for all religions equally, as all impress me as being equally hollow. . . . The happier the man, the farther he is from God.

To any man who has known the meaning of a high religion, moving from his climate into Nathan's would be like heading in for Hudson Bay. No one doubts that many virtues and satisfactions are possible in any clime, but the things which the religious man cares for most will not grow in Nathan's zone. The difference, far from being simply moral, concerns the total meaning of life, its entire feel and flavor, its cosmic outlook and spiritual climate.

The most convincing testimony on this point comes not from the religious but from the irreligious. Mr. Clarence Darrow is one of our most vocal atheists. To him the "outstanding fact" of human life is the "utter futility of it all"; he thinks that possibly "no life is of much value, and that every death is little loss" to the world; he feels that the "most satisfying part of life is the time spent in sleep, when one is utterly oblivious to existence" and "the next best is when one is so absorbed in activities"—like poker games—"that one is altogether unmindful of self." Rapidly accumulating testimony bears witness that such futilism is one of irreligion's commonest effects. To argue from atheism to badness is false in both fact and theory, but to argue from atheism to depressed enthusiasm about living is plain sailing. Professor Malinowski, one of our leading scientific agnostics, says, "Modern agnosticism is a tragic and shattering frame of mind." Well, a universe which came from nowhere save fortuitous atomic maneuvering and goes nowhither save back to it again, and in which "that nervous speck of star dust we call man" is a momentary inadvertence, may be expected to take the shine out of existence. To be sure, if one is fortunate, one may squeeze from present experience rich and jocose juices and go swimming in them; one may even believe in immediate possibilities for human society, as the Russian communists do, be sacrificially interested in adventurous enterprises of social progress, and in general may be a good citizen and a high-minded character; but to suppose that a widespread shift from belief in a spiritually significant to belief in a spiritually meaningless universe would not flood through morale into morals is, I think, in view of the nature of the moral life, obvious rationalization. The trouble with irreligion, as Professor Montague of Columbia remarks, is that, if it is true, what we care for most is at the mercy of what we care for least, and that while this state of affairs need not lead to badness, it does lead to an "incurable sadness and loneliness."

Morals, for example, consist not alone in doing good, but in enduring hardship and wrong. The severest moral test which most of us meet lies not in doing something right, but in standing something that at first seems intolerable. The armchair philosophers who theoretically separate the good life from all extrahuman relationships might profitably face, as a working minister faces, the outrageous misfortunes which ordinary men and women are called on to endure, and might well study there the good life in terms of fortitude, constancy, patience, and heroic courage. Morals, more often than the theorist takes account of, *are* morale. Some, meeting their Armageddon in the experience of disaster, grow rebellious and petulant; some grow stoical and talk about their heads being bloody but unbowed; some become resigned and try to bend to the wind without breaking; but some lay hold on their calamity as Jesus laid hold on his Cross, and use it as the most effective instrument for good which life ever fitted to their hand. I never have seen anyone transcend calamity with such positive triumph, however, who did not have more than "morals" at his disposal. Always behind such conduct there has been a total personal response to life's meaning which could not be described in any terms less than religion.

Again, the moral life, rising to its heights, often means costly self-sacrifice. Goodness is not exhausted in any calculated management of conduct with deftness and decency; at its best it means the hazardous flinging of one's life after one's ideals. To say that this is a matter not of morals only, but of morale, is to put the case mildly, as anyone can see who will carry this discussion into the prison house where Socrates drank the hemlock, or to Golgotha where Christ died. Now, sacrificial morale can be admirably exhibited without any conscious reference to cosmic meanings, as in many a scientist searching for truth and many a soldier dying for country. Nevertheless, religion and irreligion do radically differ in the climate they create for it to grow in. Socrates, appealing from the public opinion of his generation to the public opinion of the universe— "Men of Athens, I honor and love you; but I shall obey God rather than you"—was revealing a total response to life's meaning, both human and cosmic, which produced an unconsenting, independent conscience, gave it horizon and hope, infused it with zest, and empowered it for sacrifice.

Moreover, moral living, far from being an affair of blowing on one's hands and doing good, often involves recovery from disheartening failure. Much current talk about the good life without religion treats the good life as though it were an easy matter of decent conduct, keeping on the sunny side of the law, let us say, or, as Nathan puts it, not doing a dirty trick to a friend. But what intelligent person supposes that a man changing from theism to atheism would straightway rob his neighbor's henroost or cheat at cards? There are plenty of motives for ordinary decency to be found without leaving town, much more without leaving the earth. Morals, however, are more than ordinary decency; they frequently involve taking a disintegrated, dilapidated personality, disgraced and dismayed, and making a man of him. Much prevalent cocksureness about goodness minus religion would collapse if men seriously faced such meanings in the moral life as Shakspere with his profound insight saw: "I could accuse me of such things, that it were better my mother had not borne me." In such a case, morals depend upon morale, and the shining successes of religion at its best, in producing "twice-born" men who in character failed miserably and yet in the end conquered splendidly, have been due not to supernatural codes and penalties nor to theology superimposed on ethics, but to a total response to life's meaning which put heart and hope into a whipped spirit.

Moreover, the good life is not merely nor mainly a matter of individual decision; it springs from the environment and education of one's earliest years; it is the largely unconscious response of a growing character to the practical circumstances and controlling interpretations of life by which it is surrounded. In individual experience, therefore, it is not true that we start with a good life and then imagine God as its heavenly silhouette. Many of us would testify that we started in religious homes, not with a code of morals only, but with a view of life. It was taught us from the first. We were introduced to life as a spiritual adventure in a spiritual world. Through whatever mistaken forms of theology or perverted appeals to fear may have marred the medium, the glory shone of a world where the Eternal Best was endeavoring to elicit in us the best of which we were capable. We were born into a world where not mindless matter but a purposeful

God was the background, and man was not an accident of the dust but a child of the Spirit.

To an incalculable degree our finest morals have been our response to that view of life. It gave us something to live up to; it touched our honor. Citizens of such a world, we were called on to be worthy of our citizenship—*noblesse oblige.* The whole tone of our character has been profoundly affected by that challenge and by our endeavors, however fallible, to meet it. And we know beyond peradventure that had we been introduced from the beginning to the view of life of Dreiser and France and Nathan, our total response would have been immeasurably different in morale and morals.

It seems incredible, therefore, that were the current irreligious view of life to become general, morals would not respond. The cosmos, then, would be a bleak, purposeless, ruthless physical process with man, as James Branch Cabell calls him, "a parasite infesting the epidermis of a midge among the planets." When one orients oneself in a world so conceived, one does not forthwith desire to rifle his neighbor's vault, steal his wife, or defame his reputation. The natural consequence is depressed enthusiasm about living. One tends not toward murder, but toward the dismay of Strindberg's Countess Julie: Everything is an iceberg, that drifts over the water

until it sinks. If a man has failed morally, he may well wonder whether painful recovery is either possible or worth while; if he faces outrageous adversity, he is likely to find little encouragement to heroism in a world coming from nowhere, going nowhither, and ultimately coming to nothing; if duty involves costly sacrifice, there is reason to question how worthy of such care man is—"an ape who chatters to himself of kinship with the archangels while filthily he digs for groundnuts."

That is to say, in multiplied exhibitions of expressed irreligion all around us we have indubitable evidence that it does make a difference to morale. It takes the bounce out of life, robs it of radiance, resilience, zest. It need not make life wicked; it may not even make life tragic; it makes life trivial.

Let those, therefore, who can do no better overcome this handicap and construct the good life as well as they are able on an irreligious basis. That there will be enriching results of this endeavor I do not doubt. A complete disbeliever in any spiritual meaning in the cosmos can still make the creation of beauty, or research for truth, or some special social cause, his whole effective world, and can so give himself to this concentrated ideal that all believers in God will have something to live up to if they can. The rest of us, however, are certain that such par-

tition of life's response is an artificial abstraction, and that unless we can build up a total reaction to life's meaning, as a whole, which will be both good religion and good morals, we shall be playing for mankind at large a losing ethical game.

VI

All this, however, is no complete answer to the present challenge which ethics is making to religion. If the good life is so anxious, as in certain important areas it is, to secede from its ancient union, we may be sure that something is seriously the matter with the religion from which it desires to escape. The most impressive condemnation of Christianity today is voiced, not in explicit and belligerent philosophical attack, but in the ardent desire of wide areas of thoughtful, high-minded morals to get as far away from it as possible.

The ethical ideas of the churches as a whole are narrow and negative. Among many intelligent and public-spirited people mass action of Christians in the realm of morals would be deplored in advance as a catastrophe. Some conventional respectability pushed into the center of attention; some meddlesome interference by legal enactment in the private business of the people; some lid to be clamped down and triumphantly sat upon; some hasty substitution

of soft-heartedness for hard-headedness in the solution of a public problem—such operations of ecclesiastical morals, the good work of the Federal Council of the Churches of Christ in America to the contrary notwithstanding, are widely understood to be representative of organized Christianity.

Meanwhile, men and women, sometimes of no church and no creed, are engaged in moral adventures of high import: providing coöperative substitutes for the insanity of war, blazing trails up which a blundering economic order may move toward decency, retrieving our penology from superstition and barbarism to humaneness and efficiency, putting the new science of mental hygiene at humanity's disposal, banishing with the new medicine ancient plagues our fathers prayed against but could not conquer, opening doors of educational opportunity to the nation's youth.

The final answer, therefore, to the attempted secession of morals from religion is not argument but achievement. If our religion can be made intelligently and seriously ethical, so that it becomes in fact the germinative source of our best ideals, the creator of the spiritual climate in which they thrive, their sacrificial servant and, if need be, the mother of their martyrs, then, and only then, will

the case for religion's indispensable service to morals
be convincingly won.

Meanwhile, some fine agnostics and atheists are
willy-nilly making a valuable contribution to the
future of religion. Because the roots of the religious
life are deep in the soil of morals, whoever enriches
that enriches religion even though he himself may
deny its truth. Here lies the irony of all endeavors to
separate the two: with steadfast course the good life
inevitably tends, if not in this generation, then in
the next, to become religious. Valuing goodness,
men become uneasy in believing that the Creative
Power means nothing by it; sacrificing for the fur-
therance of social ideals, men find themselves thereby
implying faith that the world is fitted for social
ideals to be fulfilled in; devoting themselves to the
service of personality, men find it difficult to believe
that personality with its endless possibilities is a cosmic inadvertence; seeking integrated experience
within themselves, men resent the inward disruption of a human life morally significant in a cosmos
morally meaningless. All passionate goodness is
forever unreconciled to an ethically senseless world.

Non-theistic humanists, trying to content themselves with thin slogans, like "Morals minus Religion," would better take the measure of this towering fact. They can have morals minus religion—for

a while. They may even lead a whole generation of intellectuals into morals minus religion; but in the end they will be hoist with their own petard. The very goodness they have achieved, the more serious it is, will the more certainly press up into religion, and religion with its sustaining resources will press back into it, and the two blend in one response to life's meaning as a whole.

Reference Notes

Page	Line	
2	15	Matthew Arnold: *Literature and Dogma*, ch. i, sec. 2, p. 46 of 1873 edition.
2	16	Edward B. Tylor: *Primitive Culture*, vol. i, p. 424.
2	17	Alfred North Whitehead: *Religion in the Making*, p. 16.
2	19	Edward Scribner Ames: quoted as "an unpublished definition" by Hedley S. Dimock in "Trends in the Redefinition of Religion," in *The Journal of Religion*, July, 1928, p. 448.
2	22	George Malcolm Stratton: *Psychology of the Religious Life*, p. 343.
2	25	Robert H. Lowie: *Primitive Religion*, Introduction, p. xvi.
3	1	Salomon Reinach: *Orpheus; A History of Religions*, p. 3 of translation from the French by Florence Simmonds.
3	3	A. Eustace Haydon: quoted by Hedley S. Dimock in "Trends in the Redefinition of Religion," in *The Journal of Religion*, July, 1928, pp. 450f.

Page	Line	
3	5	George Bernard Shaw: "In the Days of My Youth," as quoted by Houston Peterson in *Havelock Ellis, Philosopher of Love*, p. 139.
3	7	Havelock Ellis: *The New Spirit*, p. 26.
15	5	Julian S. Huxley: *Religion without Revelation*, p. 34.
16	5	Henry Nelson Wieman: *The Wrestle of Religion with Truth*, pp. 69-70, 71.
16	15	Josiah Royce: Cf. *The Philosophy of Loyalty*.
20	8	Anonymous: quoted by Burnett Hillman Streeter in *Reality; A New Correlation of Science and Religion*, p. 280.
22	11	Gwilym O. Griffith: *John Bunyan*, p. 315.
23	4	Richard Wagner: letter to Robert Franz, September 25, 1852, as quoted in *Letters of Richard Wagner*, ed. by Wilhelm Altmann, vol. i, p. 233.
26	7	Henry Nelson Wieman: *The Wrestle of Religion with Truth*, p. 2.
26	20	David Starr Jordan: *The Stability of Truth*, p. 91.
32	19	Tyssul Davis: "Summing Up," in *Religions of the Empire*, ed. by William Loftus Hare, p. 518.
36	12	Origen: "Origen Against Celsus," bk. i, ch. 37, in *The Ante-Nicene Fathers*, vol. iv, p. 412.
36	23	Justin Martyr: "The First Apology of Justin," ch. xxii, in *The Ante-Nicene Fathers*, vol. i, p. 170.
37	10	Professor Margoliouth: "An Historical Note on Islam," in *Religions of the Empire*, ed. by William Loftus Hare, p. 62.

Page	Line	
37	20	Cf. James B. Pratt: *The Pilgrimage of Buddhism*, pp. 136, 165-166, 228.
38	4	*Corpus Hermeticum in Poimandres*, xiv (xiii) ; text of R. Reitzenstein, p. 339.
38	24	Epictetus: *The Discourses of Epictetus*, ch. xiv.
39	2	*The Dhammapada*, ch. xvii, as translated by D. C. Wagiswara and K. J. Saunders in *The Buddha's Way of Virtue*, p. 55.
41	14	Ernest Renan: *The Life of Jesus*, ch. v, as translated by Charles Edwin Wilbour, p. 102.
41	25	George Bernard Shaw: *Saint Joan*, sc. v, last sentence.
44	18	James Harvey Robinson: "Religion Faces a New World," in *Harper's Monthly Magazine*, September, 1928, p. 407.
48	23	H. L. Mencken: Editorial in *The American Mercury*, May, 1928, p. 26.
48	26	H. L. Mencken: *Prejudices; Third Series*, p. 132.
48	27	*Ibid.*, p. 121.
49	2	*Ibid.*, p. 125.
49	15	Ralph Waldo Emerson: "An Address delivered before the Senior Class in Divinity College, Cambridge," in Riverside Edition of his *Complete Works*, vol. i, p. 128.
54	1	Richard St. Barbe Baker: "Beliefs of Some East African Tribes," in *Religions of the Empire*, ed. by William Loftus Hare, p. 351.
55	12	Matthew Arnold: *Literature and Dogma*, ch. ix, p. 255 of 1873 edition.
56	13	Saint Catherine of Genoa, in *Vita mirabile e dottrina santa della Beata Caterina da Genova*,

Page	Line	
85	2	James Russell Lowell: "The Present Crisis," in his *Complete Poetical Works* (Cambridge Edition), p. 68.
87	16	James Branch Cabell: *Something About Eve*, p. 127.
87	17	Warwick Deeping: *Sorrell and Son*, p. 389, Sorrell speaking.
87	21	Joseph Wood Krutch: *The Modern Temper*, p. 249.
87	26	Walter Lippmann: *A Preface to Morals*, p. 330.
88	14	Bertrand Russell: "The Free Man's Worship," in *Philosophical Essays*, p. 70.
89	11	H. Faye: *Sur l'Origine du Monde*, ch. xi, pp. 256-257.
89	22	J. Scott Haldane: *Mechanism, Life and Personality*, p. 139.
89	25	Joseph Wood Krutch: *The Modern Temper*, p. 235.
91	3	George Bernard Shaw: "Maxims for Revolutionists," section on Religion, in *Man and Superman*, p. 235.
91	15	Arthur James Balfour: *The Foundations of Belief*, p. 30.
99	3	James Thompson: "The City of Dreadful Night," viii, 10th stanza.
99	10	James H. Jeans: *Eos or The Wider Aspects of Cosmogony*, p. 69.
100	22	Warwick Deeping: *Sorrell and Son*, p. 389, Sorrell speaking.
101	7	Robert H. Gault: "The Psychologist's Introduction," in *The Mind at Mischief*, by William S. Sadler, p. ix.

Page	Line	
102	9	Quoted by R. S. and H. M. Lynd in *Middletown; A Study in Contemporary American Culture*, p. 325.
103	12	Quoted by Joseph Fort Newton in *The New Preaching*, p. 107.
108	14	Warwick Deeping: *Sorrell and Son*, p. 389, Sorrell speaking.
109	7	Everett Dean Martin: *The Mystery of Religion*, pp. 112-113.
109	21	Goncourt, Jules de: quoted by Gamaliel Bradford in *D. L. Moody: A Worker in Souls*, p. 93.
110	6	Editorial, "Enough of Scientists?" in *The Christian Register*, November 7, 1929, p. 905.
111	22	James H. Jeans: *Eos or The Wider Aspects of Cosmogony*, p. 88.
112	6	George Albert Coe: book review on *The Twilight of Christianity* by Harry Elmer Barnes, in *The World Tomorrow*, February, 1930.
113	25	Burnett Hillman Streeter: *Reality; A New Correlation of Science and Religion*, p. 10.
115	17	Joseph Wood Krutch: *The Modern Temper*, p. 14.
115	24	*Ibid.*, p. 13.
118	10	Walter B. Pitkin: *The Psychology of Happiness*, p. 285.
121	16	M. C. Otto: *Things and Ideals*, p. 263.
122	3	Joseph Royce: *The Religious Aspects of Philosophy*, p. 471.
127	13	A. G. Tansley: *The New Psychology and its Relation to Life*, p. 161.

Page	Line	
128	7	James Martineau: quoted by R. H. Strachan in *The Authority of Christian Experience*, p. 45.
132	7	Hermann von Helmholtz: *Die Lehre von den Tonempfindungen, als Physiologische Grundlage für die Theorie der Musik.*
132	26	Ignace Paderewski: quoted by P. J. Philip in "Paderewski Holds Age is Against Art," in *The New York Times*, July 1, 1930.
136	27	John Keats: "On First Looking into Chapman's Homer."
139	14	Anecdote recorded by John Ruskin in a footnote to §8 of *Modern Painters*, pt. ii, sec. ii, in his *Complete Works*, Library Edition, vol. 3, p. 286.
142	8	Percy Bysshe Shelley: "A Defence of Poetry," 9th paragraph from end.
142	10	Elmer Davis: "God without Religion," in *Harper's Monthly Magazine*, March, 1930.
144	14	William Pepperell Montague: *Belief Unbound*, p. 72.
145	11	Percy Bysshe Shelley: "Adonais," liv.
145	20	Harry Elmer Barnes: *The Twilight of Christianity*, ch. viii.
148	17	Anecdote related by Theodore Gerald Soares in *Religious Education*, p. 70.
148	25	Auguste Rodin: *Art*, ch. xi.
150	12	James H. Jeans: *The Universe Around Us*, p. 318.
150	23	Leslie Stephen: *An Agnostic's Apology*, p. 5.
151	8	Albert Einstein in report of his address at Nottingham, England, as given by Edwin L. James in *The New York Times*, June 7, 1930.

Page Line
151   14   Walter Lippmann: *A Preface to Morals*, pp.
           96-97.
153   10   James H. Jeans: *The Universe Around Us*,
           p. 318.
153   16   Walter Lippmann: *A Preface to Morals*, p. 22.
155   7   Robert Louis Stevenson: *An Inland Voyage*,
           chapter on "The Oise in Flood."
157   1   David Masson: quoted by John Kelman in *The
           Faith of Robert Louis Stevenson*, pp. 224-225.
161   15   Increase Mather: "Heaven's Alarm to the
           World," as quoted by Andrew D. White in
           *A History of the Warfare of Science with
           Theology in Christendom*, vol. i, p. 195.
162   3   F. L. Mortimer: *The Peep of Day*, as quoted by
           Esmé Wingfield-Stratford in *Those Earnest
           Victorians*, pp. 208-209.
164   4   John Greenleaf Whittier: "Revelation," in his
           Complete Works, Cambridge Edition, p. 466.
164   15   Robert G. Ingersoll: Epigram heading chapter
           "The Gods," in his *Works*, New Dresden Edi-
           tion, p. 7.
167   6   George Eliot: *Adam Bede*, ch. xvii, Adam
           speaking.
168   6   Theodore Dreiser: *Living Philosophies*, ed. by
           H. G. Leach, pp. 57, 62, 74.
169   22   George John Romanes: *A Candid Examination
           of Theism by Physicus*, last paragraph.
170   20   Ralph Waldo Emerson: "Threnody," in *Poems*,
           vol. ix of his *Complete Works*, Concord Edi-
           tion, p. 157.
171   21   Anatole France: quoted by J. J. Brousson in
           Anatole France Himself, p. 65.

Page	Line	
173	4	Thomas Hardy: *The Dynasts; A Drama of the Napoleonic Wars,* pt. 3, After Scene, p. 358.
173	16	Quoted from *The Harvard Alumni Bulletin,* February 7, 1924, by Raymond Calkins in *The Eloquence of Christian Experience,* p. 6.
175	14	William Ernest Hocking: *The Self; Its Body and Freedom,* p. 45.
177	25	George Jean Nathan in *Living Philosophies,* ed. by H. G. Leach, pp. 222, 223, 227, 230, 231.
178	25	Clarence Darrow: *The Story of My Life,* pp. 449, 450, 36.
179	13	Professor Malinowski in *Science and Religion; A Symposium* (with a foreword by Michael Pupin), p. 70.
179	17	Irwin Edman in *Living Philosophies,* ed. by H. G. Leach, p. 279.
180	9	William Pepperell Montague: *Belief Unbound,* p. 67.
181	27	Socrates in "Apology," in *The Dialogues of Plato,* as translated by B. Jowett, vol. iii, p. 118.
182	12	George Jean Nathan in *Living Philosophies,* ed. by H. G. Leach, p. 229.
182	25	William Shakspere: "Hamlet, Prince of Denmark," act iii, sc. i, Hamlet speaking.
184	19	James Branch Cabell: *Beyond Life,* p. 318.
184	27	August Strindberg: *Miss Julie,* p. 13 of translation in The Modern Library of the World's Best Books.
185	8	James Branch Cabell: Quoted by V. L. Parrington in *The Beginnings of Critical Realism in America,* p. 338.

Index of Proper Names

~ 199 ~

Romanes, George J., 169
Royce, Josiah, 16, 122
Russell, Bertrand, 68, 88, 108, 163

Savonarola, 161
Shaftesbury, Anthony A. C., 55
Shakspere, William, 79-80, 182
Shaw, George Bernard, 3, 41, 91
Shelley, Percy B., 142, 145
Socrates, 181-182
Sophocles, 138
Sperry, Willard L., 81
Starbuck, Edwin D., 17
Stephen, Leslie, 150
Stevenson, Robert L., 155
Stratton, George M., 2
Streeter, Burnett H., 113

Strindberg, August, 184
Sunday, "Billy," 1

Tennyson, Alfred, 141
Thompson, Francis, 25
Toscanini, Arturo, 132, 147
Turner, William, 139
Tylor, Edward B., 2

Voliva, 1, 114

Wagner, Richard, 23, 24, 25
Whitehead, Alfred North, 1, 2, 26, 156
Whittier, John G., 164
Wieman, Henry N., 16, 26

Zoroaster, 36